The Story of GLO Europe

Stephen McQuoid

2024

Previously published as 'Vision for Mission' 2014
Revised and expanded 2024 by GLO Publishing
78 Muir Street, Motherwell, Scotland ML1 1BN

28 27 26 25 24 / 5 4 3 2 1

British Library Cataloguing in Publication Data
A catalogue record for this book is available from the British Library.

ISBN 978-0-9553051-6-0

Typeset and cover design by ProjectLuz.com
Printed and bound in Great Britain
For GLO Publishing
by Bell & Bain Ltd, Glasgow

Dedication

This book is dedicated to all the people over the past 50 years who have participated in any way in the ministry GLO Europe whether by praying, giving, volunteering, encouraging, going on a mission team or becoming a GLO Europe missionary. Whether your name is mentioned in this book or not, you share in this story with us if you have, in whatever way, supported what God has been doing through GLO Europe. Take encouragement that God sees everything we do.

Contents

The Story of GLO Europe

Whenever I am asked to describe what GLO is all about, one word comes readily to mind – mission. GLO is about mission! I firmly believe that mission is important and that if we as Christians are to obey Christ's Great Commission we must all embrace it. It was for this reason that I joined GLO as a twenty-four-year-old in 1990. It is also my personal commitment to mission that drove me to write the first edition of this book in March 2015 and also this updated version. I wanted to tell the story of GLO and all those dedicated people who have been part of the GLO story as we have tried to reach our fellow Europeans for Christ. I have deliberately focused on GLO Europe. GLO is a worldwide mission movement that has headquarters and training centres in various parts of the globe. However it is GLO Europe that I am part of and that I wish to describe in this book and for good reason. Europe today is a spiritually dark place and Europeans are deeply resistant to the gospel. Europe is not a glamorous mission destination and missionaries who go elsewhere, especially to the Majority World, often get more profile. However, it would be hard to find another part of the world where the spiritual needs are greater than Europe. It is for this reason our focus remains on this great and diverse continent. It is in this needy part of the world that I have had the privilege of working alongside Christian missionaries within the fellowship of GLO who have been heroic in their commitment to mission.

Writing history is never easy. The challenge lies not just in telling the story, but also in making sure that all the necessary details get included. Inevitably it is impossible to do justice to a story such as the history of GLO Europe, in just one small book. It is not possible to record every event, talk about every significant person and every incident. A lot of information is left out, including information that is important and meaningful. This is why lots of histories are written, each successive one making up for what has not been previously recorded. To whatever extent this book is a deficient history of GLO Europe, I offer my apologies.

Writing the first edition of this book was challenging, partly because it had to be done quickly and partly because no other history has ever been published about GLO Europe so I had to rely almost entirely on interviews, Board minutes and Spearhead magazines for my information. Some of the people I needed to interview lived on the other side of the world, so I had to make do with emails. The thinking was that people who never had any access to the first edition could still learn about the history of GLO Europe. Time pressures are the only excuse I have for reproducing a book that is still brief and limited in scope and depth (though that can also be an advantage). It is, however, a book that needed to be written and then updated because of all the things that God is still doing through the work of GLO Europe. This is a thrilling account of ordinary people who have done extraordinary things in the cause of mission.

I wish once more to thank all the people I spoke to and who gave me information for the first edition. They include Cynthia Naismith, John Speirs, Robert Kilpatrick, John Hunter, Ray and Eunice Cawston, Marion Mathers, Geoff and Janet Ruston, Alan Carmichael, John Lewis, Valerie Kyle, David Goold, Nelson Logan, Colin MacPhie, David Buchan, John Stanfield, Helen Houston, Sam Gibson, Jan Goodall, Allison Hill, Ian Smith, Philippe Perrilliat, Robert Hamilton, Mike Packer, Patrizio Zucchetto, Angie Isac and many others. In the first edition a special thanks went to Allison Hill and Adi Harris who proof-read my text and gave such good advice. Sadly Adi passed away in 2017 and is receiving his eternal reward. Allison however is still here and reproofed the second edition, for which I am grateful.

Writing this book was a labour of love the first time and more so second time around. I have now spent more of my life as a GLO worker than I have not being a GLO worker. It is an organisation I deeply appreciate because I appreciate and value the people in it. I believe God has done great things through GLO and will continue to do so. As I researched for the second edition of the book I was inspired all over again by the many pioneers in GLO who sacrificed much so that people in Europe could hear the gospel. I also felt the privilege of being able to work in the GLO Centre with its administration department, college, coffee shop and bookshop and to work alongside a whole range of people who love God and care about the spiritual needs of our world. This book (both editions) is dedicated to all the staff, GLO workers, and volunteers in the Centre as well as all the missionaries all over Europe who serve God through the ministry of GLO.

I hope one day that someone will write an adequate history of GLO. Perhaps that person may even replace me as General Director of the work of GLO, something I pray for regularly. In the meantime it is my prayer that others will also be inspired by reading this book in its second edition and see the passion for mission that is a characteristic of GLO people.

Stephen McQuoid
December 2023

Chapter 1

A Man on a Mission

History is made by people with vision and there are countless examples that bear this out. This is certainly true when it comes to the history of GLO. Now a mission organisation with Centres in more than half a dozen countries, GLO began in Australia in the mid-1960s as a result of the vision of one extraordinary man who I never had the privilege of meeting, but someone whose life has impacted me along with many others. His name was Colin Tilsley.

Colin's parents, Crawford and Marjorie Tilsley were missionaries who began their career in India in 1920. Consequently, Colin came into the world in the Lutheran Mission Hospital in Rajahmundry, south-east India. While he had a happy childhood he also experienced the challenge of separation from his parents at the tender age of five to attend Hebron, a boarding school for missionary children in Ootacamund. It was there that he became a Christian thanks to the evangelistic efforts of another missionary to India, Bob Stokes.

In 1947 Colin's parents returned to England with him and his sister Heather and once again this meant boarding school, this time in Kent. His parents furloughed in England for one year before returning to India and it would be another five and a half years before he would see them again. He used his school holidays to visit family members around the country and it was on one of these school holidays he took the step of being baptised at Alma Road Chapel in Bristol.

Cynthia

Tilsley was not naturally academic, he much preferred to play sports and he enjoyed a high level of fitness, however he did well enough at school to gain entry into a business studies course at the London School of Economics (LSE). Things were shortly about to change because Colin met his wife Cynthia, a nurse in Largs, Scotland in 1953. Cynthia was Australian but had been visiting the UK. The couple knew that they were to be together, but they would have to wait as Colin had to do his two years of National Service in the British Army. Cynthia returned to Australia and once Colin had finished his National Service he set off for Australia to marry her. However two events that were to influence Colin's life would take place before his wedding.

The first of these was the visit of evangelist Billy Graham to London in 1954 to preach at the Harringay Arena and Wembley Stadium. Colin attended the meetings and as a result he had become convinced of the value and the need for mass evangelism.

Secondly, on his way to Australia he took a four-month detour to India so he could see his parents again. This visit proved to be an equally decisive moment in his life and he was deeply challenged about the spiritual needs of the world as he witnessed the challenging situation his parents were working in. Both these experiences were to weigh on Colin's mind as he arrived in Australia.

Colin and Cynthia married on 24th August 1957 and over the next eight years they were blessed with four children. Life was good for the Tilsleys and

Cynthia & Colin Tilsley

they felt very settled, not least because Colin had a good job at the Cadbury-Fry-Pascall factory in Hobart. However, this was soon to change with a turn of events that would take them in a very different direction.

As a young married couple Colin and Cynthia began to develop a burden for full-time Christian ministry. An evangelist by the name of Gordon Blair visited their church to conduct a mission and they shared their thoughts about this with him. Blair suggested that the best pathway into full-time Christian service was to go to Bible college. The Emmaus Bible School had just opened in Sydney so Colin and Cynthia sold their house in Tasmania and went to Sydney so that Colin could complete the Bible school's two-year course.

Living conditions at Emmaus were far from luxurious for the couple, especially now that they had a two-year-old daughter in tow. Their home was little more than a glorified tin shed. To further complicate life Cynthia had a difficult pregnancy with their eldest son Alan and so spent three months of that year in bed. It was a valuable time, however, and in addition to his studies Colin also acted as Office Manager for the Bible school as well as teaming up with fellow student Russell Byard to sing duets at church services and even cut a 12" LP called 'Missionary Melodies'.

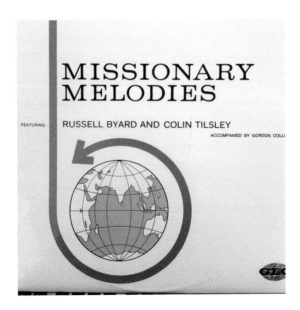

Missionary Melodies LP

When Colin graduated from Emmaus in 1961 he was appointed the Manager of the Emmaus Correspondence School. This gave him a real passion for literature work and a conviction that it could prove highly effective as an evangelistic tool. He combined this with working as a director of the 'Voice of Melody and Bible School of the Air', a Christian radio station that operated out of Sydney. Many of the programmes produced were used internationally by larger radio ministries such as HCJB and TWR. Colin became the Australian representative of the Far East Broadcasting Company. All of this was to be a useful preparation for what was to come.

Beginnings of GLO

In 1965 Colin founded Gospel Literature Outreach whose aims were to reach mass population areas with the gospel using every means possible and to handle intensive follow-up programmes. This would be done by working with resident missionaries as well as national workers and also by giving young people actual missionary experience through short-term mission teams. Later on, GLO would also introduce training so that workers could be prepared in-house for service.

Initially teams of missionaries were assembled and sent out to strategic cities for periods of between two and a half and three and a half years. This was largely based on the model set by Literature Crusades, though Colin saw it as a profoundly biblical way to do mission, citing Jesus' and Paul's ministries as examples. The first team began in Madras in 1966. Colin challenged ten young Christians to move there to perform what could only be described as a hugely challenging task, selling half a million gospel portions in this developing country over a period of two years.

This was a different way of doing mission for the churches with which Colin and Cynthia were connected and some elders had misgivings and questioned whether the project would take off while others expressed significant opposition. None of this deterred Colin, neither was he put off by questions about money, equipment or personal safety. Indeed, he took great encouragement from a letter his father wrote to him stating that he should, 'Have a big faith because you are related to a big God'.

First GLO Team to Madras

Within a short time the work had expanded to every continent of the world except North America. Colin and Cynthia focused on establishing home bases, adding Britain and New Zealand to the original one in Australia. Their strategy was to move home again and again so as to build and consolidate strong bases in different locations. While in these locations Colin would conduct a very busy preaching and teaching ministry which would make contacts and open doors. He was also a gifted administrator and so was able to run a self-contained office in addition to his itinerant ministry. This deliberate policy would bear almost immediate fruit. From 1967 to 1968 they lived in Whakatane, in the Bay of Plenty, New Zealand. Then from 1971 to 1974 they lived in Bournemouth, England and it is here that the story of GLO Europe begins.

As the work of GLO grew, it also developed as Colin responded to needs as they were identified to him. After a couple of years of GLO operating these two-year campaigns, someone approached Colin and said that they would not be able to give two years, but if GLO organised shorter teams then they would be prepared to go. The result was the commencement of what Colin called 'holiday crusades' and these became a significant part of GLO strategy especially in Europe.

Tragic news

Colin's passion for mission and his ability to relate to people and inspire them raised the profile of GLO wherever he went. He continued to travel widely spreading the vision, stirring up a greater missionary interest in churches and his gruelling schedule included preaching up to 500 times a year. Life seemed complete with a loving and supportive family as well as a fulfilling ministry, however devastation was just around the corner. The year was 1977 and Colin was planning to leave Australia for three months to travel all over the UK, the Faroe Islands, the United States and Canada speaking at conferences and missionary meetings.

For some time he had been aware of feelings of weakness and in the January of that year following a two month preaching tour of India his legs completely gave way as he chased his dog Rani and he fell heavily. Despite these difficulties Colin kept going and travelled to New Zealand in April for further meetings and to visit missionaries. A problem arose which Colin had to respond to and during a fairly intense meeting he found that his knees began shaking uncontrollably.

Once again Colin kept going, but just prior to another three-month trip, his walking deteriorated rapidly and his knees began to ache. He attended a chiropractor and then an orthopaedic specialist who stated that he was baffled by the situation. Colin expressed his concern to Cynthia stating that he might not be able to cope with the three-month tour in this condition.

Coincidently he was seeing his own family doctor at the time for inoculations for his trip and he mentioned his concern about his legs. The doctor sent Colin to a leading Macquarie Street neurologist who gave him foreboding answers to his questions. When Colin asked, 'is it serious?' the neurologist answered, 'yes'. Colin then asked, 'how serious?' to which the answer came back, 'it is very serious'. Worst of all the neurologist stated, 'There is no treatment and there is no known cure', a tragedy for a man of only forty-two who had a burning desire to serve God.

The problem was the spinal nerve disease known as Motor Neurone Disease. It deteriorates the motor nerves inside the spinal cord which leads to muscle atrophy and eventually total paralysis. Colin was devastated at the news and within a couple of days was in hospital to have extensive tests. These only confirmed the diagnosis and Colin was told that he had only three years to live and that bit by bit he would become gradually weaker and eventually totally paralysed.

The trip had to be cancelled and like never before Colin had to learn to rely on God in this greatest of all crisis. Cynthia and the whole family were equally devastated, with Colin describing his condition as a death sentence. Over the next few days and nights he and Cynthia spent many hours praying together and reading the Psalms. As a couple they were to discover God in a new way through the Psalms, especially Psalms 6, 18, 23, 56, 57, 61, 73 and 102.

Upon Colin's release from hospital a friend urged him to try alternative forms of treatment, so he went to Melbourne and received extensive acupuncture treatment which temporarily alleviated some of the symptoms, but it was short lasting. As news of Colin's condition spread, many friends phoned to express their concern and hundreds of letters also poured in. This was a comfort but could not remove the anguish about what lay ahead.

Colin continued in ministry, leading Bible studies on a mission team in Kiama, New South Wales in January of 1978. During the team he and Cynthia returned briefly to Sydney for an appointment with another neurologist, but the diagnosis was still the same. It was heart-breaking, but the couple somehow knew that God was in control of the situation.

Colin's symptoms began to manifest themselves with substantial weight loss and significant weakness and he was only able to walk with the aid of a stick. The frustration of weakness was particularly marked because he had previously been so fit. He continued to try a variety of remedies as well as altering his diet, but nothing could halt the inevitable! As he grew weaker, he spent his afternoons in bed and used the time to study the Bible. Then came periods of anxiety and introspection as he reflected on the purpose of suffering. At no time did he blame God for what had happened, but he asked himself whether he was being purified by the ordeal.

Against doctors' advice he kept going, travelling to Tasmania that March to speak at a conference, a camp and to lecture at the GLO Training Centre in Smithton. At the conference he had to sit to preach and at one of the teaching sessions at the camp he tripped over some microphone leads and fell heavily. He eased the obvious tension by telling a joke and while these events were difficult for him physically, they were a blessing to those who were there. Most of all he enjoyed lecturing at the GLO Training Centre which reminded him of the importance of his own training.

Next Colin travelled with Cynthia to New Zealand to the GLO Training Centre in Te Awamutu where he lectured again and spoke at a large conference. It was physically demanding but his burden to enthuse others with mission drove him on relentlessly despite his ever-increasing weakness. The students, most of whom were young people, were inspired both by Colin's courage and Cynthia's commitment both to Colin and to her faith as she cared for him.

Colin was soon confined to a wheelchair which in itself was a major mental battle. A house fire contributed to his trials as did the increased debilitation. He reached a point where he could barely hold anything and had to be continually nursed by Cynthia. Finally in 1981 his ordeal came to an end as he received his heavenly reward at the age of just forty-six. His life had touched many and his influence lives on in various parts of the world, including Europe, one of the places where GLO continues to operate.

Chapter 2

The Birth of GLO Europe

Having lived in New Zealand from 1967–1968 spreading the vision, Colin and Cynthia along with their family moved to the UK and lived in Bournemouth from 1971–1974. Colin's purpose in the UK was the same as it had been in New Zealand - to stimulate mission interest among churches and begin some evangelistic work. Europe was very much at the forefront of GLO's thinking and a two-and-a-half-year team had already been initiated in Rome in 1970 which included Warwick and Ozvalda Malcolm and Ron and Eunice Diprose who were to remain in Italy as missionaries long after the team had come to an end. The impact of Colin and Cynthia's time in New Zealand was already being felt with a steady stream of missionaries leaving New Zealand for Europe to work with GLO. A key couple among these were David and Jean Goold. They, along with the Hansens and Judy Arnold, left New Zealand by ship, the Achille Lauro, in February of 1971 and arrived in Genoa five and a half weeks later and then took a train on to Marseille to begin the GLO Resident Team there. They were joined a few months later by Tony and Jane Gower who had previously spent two years in Japan and later again by Dynes and Lynette McConnell, Russell and Lois Embling, Marian MacIvor from Scotland and Nora Greatbatch who came from Tasmania.

GLO in the UK

Now that he was based in the UK Colin set about motivating people to get involved in the work of GLO. Graham and Alison Black from Scotland and Margaret Davis from Colchester were the first to respond and made a two-and-a-half-year commitment to the work in France. The rationale behind a two-and-a-half-year commitment was that a missionary could spend six months in language school followed by two years of mission work. This was to prove optimistic given the length of time it takes to become proficient in a language and the difficulty of evangelism in Europe. However, it did have the benefit of encouraging potential missionaries to take the plunge knowing that the initial commitment need not be an indefinite one. It could be argued that the highly motivational style which compelled people to go out to the mission field with little by way of preparation and not much personal support was very risky, especially by today's standards. Certainly it was challenging for the missionaries and some frustration and failure were inevitable. However, there was a pioneering spirit about GLO and Colin's unwavering commitment to reaching the world for Christ proved infectious and attractive.

The Blacks had already established contact with David and Jean Goold and Graham visited France in 1972 to look at the possibility of joining the mission team there having previously developed an interest in France following his experience on a short-term team. Margaret Davis had been a teacher in Leamington Spa and went to a missionary conference in Birmingham at which Colin Tilsley had been speaking and as a result she did a four-week summer team in France in 1972. This was followed by an Easter team in Malta in 1973 and while on this team she was convinced that God wanted her to go to France as a missionary. They all joined the newly formed Grenoble team along with Nora Greatbatch who moved there from Marseille.

Colin travelled extensively recruiting people for mission as well as trying to find a base for the work. He favoured London as a UK base for GLO but nothing opened up. Tilsley's style was to directly challenge people and motivate them to take the risk and enter Christian service whether for a short-term team or a longer period. There were generally three options available to interested people. They could do a 'holiday team' which usually took place at Easter or the summer months, they could commit to being on a residential team for a two-and-a-half-year period or they could enter full-time Christian work with an open-ended commitment.

A magazine called Spearhead began to be produced so that team reports could be published and opportunities for mission promoted. It had a simple format and utilised rudimentary production techniques. As the name suggested, Spearhead was designed to challenge Christians to get involved in the frontline of evangelism. Colin was happy to recruit from anywhere; he just longed to see people take up the challenge of communicating the gospel. With the Tilsleys living in Bournemouth and missionaries such as the Goolds in France, Europe now began to feature prominently in its content. The first edition of the 1973 Spearhead showed a photo of David Goold giving literature to a woman in a small French town. It also advertised a two-and-a-half-year team for Grenoble in France along with short-term teams to Le Havre, Chartres and Grasse in France as well as short teams to Malta and Rome.

Early contact

GLO had little by way of structure in the early days, it was very much mission in the raw. The strategy was to find an important location, a country or a city and, invited by a local church, to cover the area with literature. Other methods of evangelism such as open-air preaching were also used. By the time that GLO became established in the UK in 1974, there were already 58 full-time GLO workers worldwide, including in France and Italy. The GLO style was not to talk about mission but to do it! There was an energy and passion about the work and so it tended to attract risk takers, visionaries and mavericks.

One of the people Colin came in contact with during his time in the UK was Fred Kelling, a lecturer in aerodynamics at Glasgow University. Fred had a deep burden for the remote Faroe Islands as well as European countries that lay behind the Iron Curtain. Fred made frequent trips into Eastern Europe to encourage Christians there. Colin went on one of these trips with Fred in 1973 travelling some 5,000 miles in the process. It was an eventful trip as the pair were held at gunpoint for four hours while their luggage was searched and the Bibles and New Testaments they took with them were confiscated. Colin was nevertheless grateful that no further action was taken given that only months earlier a Protestant minister was jailed for two years for taking Bibles behind the Iron Curtain. Undeterred by the setback they were able to preach in several churches, meet with groups of elders and also pass on gifts and clothing to the beleaguered but grateful Christians. The trip only served to increased Colin's burden for Europe and also convinced Fred of the merits of GLO.

The years 1973 and 1974 saw the green shoots of what was to eventually become GLO Europe. Fred began to think about developing a training ministry in the UK. Meanwhile two long-standing friends, Robert Kilpatrick and John Speirs began to think about how they could get involved in the work of GLO. Robert and John shared an involvement in the Hamilton Missionary Fellowship, affectionately known as the HMF. This was a youth missionary meeting that was started by Jim and Sadie Hislop, initially in their home in June of 1962 when they invited a missionary, Henry Beicht, to come and speak to the six young people who were invited. This format continued with other missionaries on furlough being invited to come and talk about their ministry and then the young people would pray about the needs that were highlighted. As the HMF grew the venue changed several times until finally the organisers acquired a permanent building, a wooden hut in Hope Street, Hamilton, opposite the bus station. By this time around 100 young people were attending every Friday night and this was proving to be a huge impetus for mission in Central Scotland. Both Robert and John became leaders in the HMF and worked together in it.

John Speirs & Robert Kilpatrick

Robert and his wife Eileen began to feel a real burden for literature ministry and Robert was thinking about giving up his job as a sales representative so he could go into full-time Christian service. He had written to Literature Crusades asking advice on the issue and they suggested he should contact Colin Tilsley. Robert did so and Colin dropped into Glasgow on his way to Aberdeen for a chat with Robert. This conversation greatly influenced Robert and he felt that joining GLO was the right move for him. They kept in contact and Colin was later invited back to speak at the HMF.

The work begins

Robert and Eileen were commended in 1973 from Selkirk Street Evangelical Church in Hamilton and became the first full-time GLO workers from Europe. At the commendation service Colin Tilsley was the speaker. At the end of the service Colin Tilsley challenged John Speirs and said, 'we need you in the work', a challenge that was to bear fruit the following year. After his commendation Robert Kilpatrick began doing door-to-door work in Hamilton and tried to encourage the young people in the HMF to get involved in evangelism. He also began organising short-term teams using the same group of young people.

Another of Robert's activities was to sell Bibles and books door-to-door. Feeling this ministry could be extended he looked for a premises in the town of Hamilton. Robert, John and a friend, George Falconer, acquired a minibus and drove to the STL (Send the Light which was a UK Christian book distributor) warehouse in London, filled the van with books and held a Christmas bookstall for the four weeks of December 1973 at the Hamilton Missionary Fellowship centre. During that month they also did some door-to-door evangelism and then found a disused chip shop in Brown Street, Hamilton (Brown Street no longer exists). It was here that the first GLO Bookshop opened on 23rd February 1974 and Robert and Eileen ran it with the help of volunteers including Sadie Hislop, Marion Lamb, Bob McDowell and Marion Mathers.

John and Cathie Speirs were next to be commended to the work of GLO Europe and this took place in October of 1974. The challenge he received from Colin Tilsley and also one from George Verwer at a conference in Birmingham 1972, convinced John that he should join GLO. That same year both Fred Kelling and David Prosser, who was from South Wales, went full-time with

GLO along with their wives. David Prosser began to attend agricultural shows to distribute literature and do evangelism. He also led short-term mission teams in Ireland. While these people focused their attention on Europe, others from the UK were inspired to join GLO and work elsewhere: this included Walter and Elizabeth Alexander from Newmains, John Axford from Bath and Jim Jardine from Burnbank, who all joined the work and went to Brazil.

The GLO Centre begins

In 1974, what is now the GLO Centre, was leased from the Church of Scotland with Colin Tilsley negotiating the terms of the lease. Colin had been looking for a premises somewhere in the Central Belt, perhaps even between Glasgow and Edinburgh, as this area was the most densely populated in Scotland. A local businessman, Wallace Kirkland, who was heavily involved in a para-church youth ministry called the Maranatha Centre, was the key contact. Wallace, along with the Maranatha Centre choir, was at a social evening at Dalziel Parish Church of Scotland in Motherwell. Dalziel Parish Church was directly adjacent to Dalziel North Church and the two congregations had recently merged leaving the premises of the North Church vacant. The minister of the Parish Church invited Wallace to meet his Kirk Session, the 86-person leadership structure of the church. At this meeting they offered Wallace the building to be used for the Maranatha Centre. Wallace felt that it was too big for his purposes but having met Colin Tilsley and having been impressed by his vision, he thought that GLO could make better use of the building.

Colin was delighted with the offer and so the former Dalziel North Church became the GLO Centre, Motherwell. As the property was large and the work was growing, it was important that GLO was registered in Scotland as a charitable trust. On one occasion when Colin was preaching at Selkirk Street, a young lawyer called John Hunter spoke to him after the service. John introduced himself to Colin stating that he was a lawyer and said, 'if there is anything I can do to help, let me know'. The next day Colin phoned John and asked him if he could do the legal work required for the securing of the buildings as well as help with establishing GLO as a charity. The premises, while in poor condition, had a great deal of potential. They consisted of a church building that could seat 800 people, two church halls, a large manse and a smaller wooden building that would later be used for a printing press and literature store. Initially the premises were leased for a ten-year period with the understanding that if GLO sold the buildings within that time they would have to give some of the proceeds back to the Church of Scotland. This was a way of ensuring that GLO wouldn't just buy the property cheaply and then make a quick profit.

GLO Centre

The bookshop in Brown Street was moved into the foyer of the church building within the new GLO Centre. A friend, Graham Scholefield, was working in the Glasgow department store and they were doing some refurbishing. He offered some shelving free of charge for use in the bookshop. Robert Kilpatrick ran the bookshop and also began a printing ministry so that tracts could be produced for distribution by GLO teams. He also acted for a time as Secretary for the GLO Centre in Motherwell.

The large manse which was part of the church complex and was split in two. Fred and Ruth Kelling moved into the upstairs flat that had been created and Robert and Eileen Kilpatrick lived downstairs.

Book ministry

Send The Light (STL), had a desire to provide a nationwide book wholesale service but their geographic location made it difficult for them to supply the North of England and Scotland. Gerry Davey the head of STL visited Motherwell and asked if GLO would be willing to be the wholesale provider for these locations. After extensive negotiations it was agreed that the GLO Bookshop could purchase books at a 35% reduction and GLO could have 15% from any wholesale books they sold. Again, Robert ran the wholesale business, spending one week out of every month on the road visiting Christian bookshops. This activity provided a great deal of funding for the fledgling GLO Europe and supported by many volunteers, helped make the bookshop ministry a reality.

This work continued and was eventually taken over by Geoff and Janet Ruston when they joined GLO. Many years later when STL moved their warehouse to Carlisle there was no need for a distribution depot in Motherwell. STL realised that this would have financial implications for GLO and so they gave a generous gift in compensation.

GLO Committee

As the work began to come together a Committee was formed at the end of 1974 to give some structure and a sense of permanence to the work. The first Committee members were: David Prosser, John Speirs, Walter Baxter, WK Morrison, George Willcocks, Robert MacPhie, Robert Kilpatrick, Jimmy Black and Fred Kelling. With no lawyer on the Committee and John Hunter taking responsibility for GLO's legal work, he also sat in on some of the early Committee meetings though he was not at that time a Committee member. Fred Kelling was Secretary to the Committee until 1982 at which point John Speirs took over.

The choice of Committee members was deliberate and it included some of the early full-time GLO workers, but Colin also wanted to bring on board men who already had stature within Scottish churches as they would be able to lend their personal kudos to what was a completely new enterprise. It also spoke volumes for Colin's motivational qualities and his ability to convey a vision.

GLO was entirely new to Scotland and the idea of mission being organised rather than missionaries simply being 'spirit led' was novel at the time.

First GLO Committee Left to right: David Prosser, John Speirs, Walter Baxter, Willie Morrison, George Willcocks, Robert MacPhie, Robert Kilpatrick, Jimmy Black, Fred Kelling

Furthermore, teamwork was not a feature of mission in those days, missionaries were supposed to be rugged individualists relying only on God. Colin managed to convince all of these men of the merits of GLO and its methods and encourage them to make their contribution.

Beginning training

The following year Fred Kelling began the GLO Training Course. The main church hall building had a large room which was partitioned to provide dormitory style bedrooms. A basic lecture room was also created by portioning off a section of the room. It was very rough and ready, but it was a start. Fred's idea was that if even one person came along he would enrol them on the course and train them.

Ad hoc ministry

John Speirs and Robert Kilpatrick worked together, each doing missions in local churches, preaching night by night. A Spearhead magazine from 1974 advertised John as being available, 'for evangelistic campaigns and meetings throughout the country, as invited'. They also assembled short-term teams in different parts Scotland, often on holiday weekends to do open-airs and mass literature distribution. These teams were the front-line of evangelism and they relied on the local churches to do the follow up work.

With things coming together in the UK it was time to launch some mission teams into Europe. Robert had led a team to Naples in 1973 at which a huge amount of literature was distributed, open-airs were conducted as well as a children's mission. His friendship with Fares Marzone was a key link for the development of the Italian work. However long-term mission work was still primarily the preserve of the New Zealand and Australian missionaries who had come over in the early 1970s and those people who had been personally contacted by Colin Tilsley. UK missionaries who joined them were in the minority. Consequently, with the exception of that first Naples team, any short-term teams in Europe were by and large coordinated by the New Zealand missionaries who were resident in France and Italy with David Goold being asked to co-ordinate all the French field activity.

A key part of the early work was the help of volunteers. The bookshop relied heavily on volunteers and when Cathie Speirs started up a coffee shop, also in the church building of the GLO Centre, she too relied on voluntary help. Many of these volunteers were to spend years helping GLO in whatever way they could, and some long-term volunteers eventually became GLO workers in their own right or entered full-time Christian service with other organisations.

Clive and Jane Govier then joined the work and Clive spent a great deal of time touring the country speaking in churches and reporting on the work of GLO. They continued this until they emigrated to Smithton, Tasmania so that Clive could take up the principalship of the Training Centre there.

Original coffee shop

First full year

The year 1975 was a defining one! It was the first full year of operations with bookshop, evangelistic teams and training all running. It was also a year of frenetic activity. Andy Speirs led a team of 50 people based in the GLO Centre and evangelised all over Motherwell. John Speirs and Robert Kilpatrick, along with their wives Cathie and Eileen, led two teams back-to-back to Rome to coincide with Holy Year. These teams had a total of 100 people on them. The two couples drove to Rome while some of the team flew, and they all stayed in a Baptist Centre in the city. In Rome they linked up with Dan Pasquale and Warwick Malcolm. The team included Eleanor Machray (later to join GLO), Senga Wood (who later married Keith Lake and they spent many years as missionaries in Congo prior to Senga joining the GLO Board), Alan Gamble who met his wife (Elizabeth Waugh) on the team and Brian Waites. During the team they distributed 300,000 pieces of literature – a tract called 'Holy Year' which had been written by a converted Jesuit Priest.

Team to Rome 1975

It was at this point that a serious health issue struck John Speirs. John emerged from the catacombs in Rome coughing up blood. On his return to Scotland, he consulted a doctor only to discover he had contracted tuberculosis. He spent three months as a patient in the Udston Hospital and a further three months convalescing at home.

Despite the remarkable growth of the work in Europe and elsewhere, Colin Tilsley's appetite for further growth continued to be voracious. In a memo to past team members printed in a Spearhead in 1975 he appealed for 1,000 workers to staff the many summer teams that were being planned. He also stated the need for long-term workers including secretaries for both the Sydney and Motherwell offices and a printer for Motherwell.

Tragic news

Colin had planned to return to the UK in 1979 but tragically this was not to be. On one particular day Robert Kilpatrick got a telegram from Australia to say that Colin Tilsley had been diagnosed with motor neurone disease. Everyone was shocked by the news because they all hoped and believed that the work of GLO would grow specifically because of the dynamism and energy of Colin Tilsley. Instead, in the sovereignty of God, it grew through his untimely death. The workers who were left would need to learn to develop the work on their own, albeit that each of them had been impacted by the life of this remarkable man.

Kirkcaldy Centre

When Geoff and Janet Ruston joined GLO, they soon took over the book ministry with Janet running the Motherwell bookshop and Geoff the wholesale distribution. Geoff also became treasurer, a logical choice given his background in banking. At this point things within GLO Europe began to formalise with more established roles being set up. The Committee was also strengthened in 1984 with the addition of John Hunter, and a businessman from Kirkcaldy called Norman Rollo. John had already been heavily involved in the work of GLO carrying out all the legal work while his wife Rae was a long-term volunteer in the GLO Coffee Shop. John Hunter was to remain on the Board for 27 years and would be the Chairman of GLO for many of those years.

In that same year a new venture was commenced in Kirkcaldy, a seaside town of 50,000 people in Fife, in the East of Scotland. John Speirs had been doing missions with churches in the area and Geoff, with his wholesale distribution ministry, had also become familiar with the area and churches there. All of this coincided with a local businessman, John Lewis, resigning from his directorship of an expanding company so that he could focus his energies on a literature ministry. At the same time, Denise Girling who worked in the Motherwell bookshop was engaged to someone from Kirkcaldy and was open to help in a new venture there. A property was found just off the High Street which could accommodate a bookshop, coffee shop, meeting room and resource centre. After weeks of negotiation a good price for the property was agreed and that summer the new Centre was opened. John Lewis was to play a key role in the early days of the Kirkcaldy Centre. So too was Gwen McDowell (now Gwen Purdie) who joined the work from Edinburgh in 1985 to establish what was to become a very effective counselling ministry.

GLO Kirkcaldy

1985 also became a landmark year for GLO Europe for another reason. Up until this point the main vehicle for communicating GLO news to churches was the Spearhead magazine which was produced in Australia. Consequently, information about the work in Europe was sometimes submerged in information about the work all over the world. The decision was taken that from 1985 onwards, a dedicated European version of Spearhead would focus on the European work. This was an important step and gave GLO Europe a potent vehicle for the dissemination of information.

Chapter 3

Training for Service

From the very beginning training was an inherent part of the ministry of GLO. Colin Tilsley believed that potential workers could be trained within the structure of GLO and therefore be well prepared to serve as GLO workers. With training centres being established in Smithton, Australia and Te Awamutu, New Zealand, it now fell to Fred Kelling to begin the European training work in Motherwell. Now that GLO was leasing the complex in Motherwell from the Church of Scotland, facilities were now available to make this a reality.

Training begins

The programme that was established was called the 'Training for Service' Course, but it was commonly referred to by students and local people as 'the GLO Course'. From its inception in 1975 until 1982/83 it was run on more or less the same basis each year irrespective of how many students attended. The basic structure consisted of a series of one-week courses with ten of these courses making up a term and with a two-term academic year. The first term would lead up to Christmas and then the second term would begin in early January, finishing at the end of March. Generally, the same person would lecture all week and each week would be self-contained. A typical week would contain a total of 10 hours of classroom teaching. The curriculum would include biblical studies, Christian doctrine and practical ministry skills. Fred himself would teach some of the courses but would also invite visiting lecturers. The emphasis was not just to be an academic programme, but one to prepare students for evangelism and also for ministry within the local church. In many ways it would reflect Fred's own passion for evangelism.

Fred Kelling

This emphasis was evident in the course structure. In addition to the lectures, students were expected to do some practical work not only within the Training Course itself, but also in the other activities which were developing at the Centre. There was a daily devotional programme led by Fred and all students were expected to fully integrate into local church life. The closest in proximity was Roman Road Hall (now Roman Road Community Church) which became the church of choice. Students were also involved in evangelism with a weekly session of door-to-door visitation and most weeks there were open-airs in the shopping precinct in Motherwell with students being encouraged to preach. In the early days an annual trip was made to Cambridge where the students received teaching from Robert Gordon, a lecturer who would later become Regius Professor of Hebrew at Cambridge University.

An immediate impact of the course was that some of the students, after graduating, would go out to the mission field, although only some of them joined GLO. Soon former students could be found serving God in a number of countries. The risks taken by students should not be overlooked. Many left the course with very little by way of savings and no guarantee that they would be supported if they launched out in mission. Despite this, the atmosphere created by the course had the effect of compelling students to commit themselves to Christian service irrespective of the uncertainties involved. Ironically some of the cross cultural workers who were now joining GLO had not done the training programme and this was corrected in due course.

Initially the course intake was small, never climbing into double figures. This was often perceived by churches and bigger training institutions as a weakness, however the depth of relationships formed during the year and the focus of real discipleship tended to suggest a different conclusion. The course was more than just an educational experience, it was a life changing event. In total 46 students completed the course during the first 8 years and 9 of these were subsequently involved in more than 3 years of full-time Christian service, and at least 5 of these remained in Christian service for many more years.

On a shoestring

The resources available to the training course were very limited and the infrastructure was extremely basic. The former church halls that sat next to the church building in the GLO Centre housed the training work. A large hall was partitioned into sections to accommodate male and female students and plastic sheeting was used to section off part of the same room for a lecture area. Fees were kept at a minimum so that in 1982 the charge for tuition and accommodation was only £25 per week which was about a third of what would have been charged at a standard Bible college.

During the 1982/83 academic year a major development took place which revolutionised life on the training programme as well as other activities at the Centre. The first phase of this refurbishment was the auditorium in the main church building. It was at this time that more space was created for the bookshop. A coffee shop was established which opened every weekday. For the training course new student bedrooms were built along with a dining room, toilet, shower and bathroom facilities and a recreation hall, all of these located in the former church halls. This hugely improved the living conditions for students though teaching facilities continued to be a problem with no proper lecture room.

New leadership

In June 1983, Ray and Eunice Cawston joined the work of GLO after many years of missionary service in Peru. Their initial role was to be house parents, a role that had already existed for several years. However, after December 1983 when Fred Kelling indicated that he would be retiring from the training work in June 1984, Ray began to assume responsibility as course leader. He was to revolutionise and shape the course adding significant value to what was already there, as well as to influence some wider GLO activity.

Although considerable improvements had been made, the facilities were still very limited. There was no lecture room, no library and no student lounge. A combined lecture room and library was built in what had been the narrow stage area of the old church halls. Old kitchen cupboards had their doors removed and were used to shelve the library books. Desks, in turn, were made from the cupboard doors and the narrowness of the room meant that students had to sit in what could only be described as a fairly cramped space. Some boxes of donated books were available and from these the useful ones formed the basis of the library collection. About 400 more were purchased through the bookshop. Denise Girling, a trained librarian, set up the beginnings of a library classification using the Dewey Decimal system. This job was later taken on by Jim Brown who was the Librarian for many years. A corner of the dining room was used as a student lounge and slightly more comfortable chairs were bought for it. The security of the buildings had to be improved and dampened door closers were also fitted throughout the ground floor area to reduce noise.

Ray Cawston

Up until 1983 the course had included a total of 200 classroom hours in two terms. From 1983/84 onwards this was extended to three terms with the third term incorporating a six-week block of structured practical experience in Christian ministry which the students did individually, and a further 40 hours of classroom lectures. After a while it became apparent that for some students and some of the placements, six weeks was too long a time, so it was reduced to a four- or five-week placement.

Other developments further strengthened and developed the course. Graham Poland accepted an invitation to join the staff alongside Ray and Eunice and was involved in the teaching and planning of the course and leading the students in evangelism and practical training. Graham's contribution during those years was invaluable. It was during this period of the Training

Centre's history that, having completed a couple of summer mission teams in Donegal, I was encouraged by the team leader, Nelson Logan, to come on the GLO course. That year, 1984, was an important year for me as it would shape and change my life and impress upon me the value of the work of GLO.

Graham Poland teaching

Developing programme

Thought was now also given to publicity and the Training Centre staff began to put a lot of effort into actively recruiting students for the course. A leaflet was prepared for wider public circulation backed up by a more substantial brochure. The number of classroom hours were increased again from 240 to 375 hours with some units extending across an entire term in addition to the ones taught on a one-week basis. Evaluated written assignments and final tests were also incorporated to add more academic rigour to the course and a few carefully chosen subjects made substantial use of student presentations based on their own research.

Practical training was also diversified, with different areas of experience being tailored for each student. This meant that during the year each student would gain some experience in children's work, youth work and an area of social care. For each practical assignment the student was allocated a tutor, who carried out an evaluation at the end of the period of work. One valuable by-product was a development of good relationships with other Christian organisations and churches in Central Scotland. The increasing sophistication of the training programme meant that a Student Handbook had to be produced fully detailing the overall programme.

Up until this point all students attended Roman Road Hall on Sundays but this changed and students were now allocated to several churches. This proved a blessing to students and churches alike and good relationships began to be developed between students and local churches. For a few years a Report Tour was organised which involved the student group travelling to a number of churches in a geographical area for a period of about ten days. They would give a standard presentation including reports, music and audio visuals about the course and the wider work of GLO. Where possible the Report Tour included a visit to the 'Echoes of Service' office (now Echoes International). This link was important to cultivate because at that time overseas GLO workers did not qualify for inclusion by Echoes so such overtures were significant. For the same reason, a member of the 'Echoes' Board was invited to Motherwell each year to speak to the students.

Dealing with reality

There was also an important need for financial accountability and good financial management across the Centre. The training course began to assume its fair share of Centre overheads and it was decided to increase fees by about 10% a year so that they would gradually approach a more realistic level. Consequently from 1982 to 1996 the annual tuition fees, accommodation and board rose from 23% to 60% of the national average for theological colleges and the weekly charge from 38% to 65% of the national average. The primary reason why fees could be kept so low was that, unlike most Bible colleges, the staff running the GLO course received no salary and visiting lecturers received only a small gift and modest travel expenses. What is more, because the Training Centre was part of a larger GLO campus, costs could be shared. Of course, students entering some UK Bible colleges could, under certain circumstances, receive a government grant. This happened for the first time in 1983 for a GLO student from Scotland. These grants continued for a number of years but only for Scottish students until the policy changed.

With the increased professionalism of the GLO course and in particular the need to demonstrate credibility to the government grants' authority, the qualifications of teaching staff were publicised in the Training Centre brochure. This move caused some discussion within GLO as some feared this might be symptomatic of a move towards a more academic and less practical course. The counter argument, which won the day, was that the Training Centre needed not only to keep up with both expectations of students who committed themselves to the course, but more importantly, it needed to demonstrate credibility to the government and other education authorities.

Another important development was that each student was also given an evaluation report, a copy of which was also sent to their supporting church leaders. A certificate was issued as evidence of the student's achievement. In the early days this certificate was issued on behalf of the church. The principle was that the local church would commend the student to GLO for training, and GLO would offer training to the student on behalf of the local church. The course continued to maintain a very practical emphasis and a Guest Week was introduced at the end of each year. During this week a Christian leader with significant experience in ministry was invited to encourage students from their own experience as well as to take part in the graduation.

In addition to the full-time residential training, a programme of seminars also began in 1984 so that people who were not able to take a year out could nevertheless have some training in relevant subjects. This opened up the opportunity for a wider group of students to benefit from the training on offer.

Development of the facilities also continued; this time the kitchen became the focus of attention. It was in poor condition and certainly very inadequate for a growing body of students. In 1983 a small legacy enabled some equipment to be purchased, and in 1985 a grant of £5000 was made by a Christian Trust which made a complete refurbishment possible enabling the kitchen to meet ever increasing Health and Hygiene requirements.

From about 1986 the decision was made to employ a cook/housekeeper, rather than depend on GLO personnel and other voluntary labour. This was an important decision because food was not an optional extra and the burden on Eunice's shoulders was enormous. The longest serving cook/housekeeper has been Heather Edwards who later moved on to join the coffee shop staff.

Phase two

In the same year a second major phase of Centre development took place. Plans had been drawn up for a new lecture room, offices and study bedrooms, together with a book warehouse and a print shop. However, the configuration of these plans was not workable, so they were abandoned and a new design was enacted. This was done by using prefabricated classroom units which were acquired from a local school and reassembled on site. This was a good example of GLO making the most of what they had because these classroom units were already reaching the end of their life expectancy, yet they are still in use today! The current main lecture room and additional accommodation wing was brought into use during the 1985/86 academic year, in addition to a student lounge which has since been repurposed. In addition the Scottish Development Agency contributed to the project with a stone cleaning and landscaping project that transformed the overall look of the GLO Centre. Not only were the buildings now sufficiently adapted to be useful, but located in a town centre surrounded by commercial activities and high-density residential areas meant it was perfectly placed for a training and mission organisation.

One of the biggest daily challenges was the lack of office space and equipment as well as secretarial assistance. These problems were gradually resolved, usually in very small steps. For example, the purchase of an electric typewriter bought with a gift from a visiting missionary and then the introduction of computers in 1988.

Graham Poland moved on in 1989 to work with Grosvenor Chapel in Barnstaple. This left a significant gap and help was needed. One of the key roles that Graham fulfilled was leading the students in evangelism and this was temporarily filled during the 1989/90 year with help from Ann Finlay. In 1990 I joined the staff on a full-time basis and was followed two years later by Allison Hill. Another important addition was David Clarkson who combined his GLO work with serving Cartsbridge Evangelical Church in Glasgow. David brought experience in Christian leadership and education.

His remit was to form the Extension Ministries department of the Training Centre which would make training more accessible to a greater number of people. One of the most significant aspects of this work was the development of the 'Learning to Lead' course which began as a seminar course based in the GLO Centre and later developed into an e-learning course and also a book with CD-Rom support package.

Introducing modules

From 1984–1990 course numbers maintained at a similar level and often the students had previous experience of higher education. Roughly half of the students during this period entered full-time Christian service following their training. However, in early summer of 1990 it was evident that enrolment was becoming a significant problem. It became clear that the course itself needed to be re-evaluated from an educational point of view.

The course was subsequently re-designed on a modular basis as it was felt this would improve it educationally, helping the students maintain focus over shorter five-week periods and also enabling part time students to participate in a single or a selection of modules if they wished. Exams were stopped and a process of formal continuous assessment began. Before this new programme was finally launched, Howel Jones who had a great deal of experience as an educationalist, was asked to evaluate the new programme and he expressed encouragement for the new programme. A change was also made in the publicity as the decision was taken to produce a larger prospectus and make it much more widely available.

A further innovation occurred in 1994 where an approach was made by Peter Grosvenor of 'Echoes of Service' proposing a Missionary Orientation Week, to which prospective Christian workers could receive some focused and specialist training. This week included a brief introduction to missiological issues such as cross-cultural communication and mission history as well as practical advice and some self-evaluation. Initially this was held in June after the training programme finished but it soon became an integrated part of the training year.

Using the term 'GLO Training Centre' had its limitations. While it was good to convey the impression that the emphasis was on training for action rather than being merely theoretical, it was a rather generic term. It was decided that that it would be better to use the term 'College' as part of the title and after a considerable amount of deliberation the new name Tilsley College was arrived at. This would link the training course firmly with its roots as a mission training centre. On 29th November 1995 Cynthia Naismith, the widow of Colin Tilsley, replied to our letter warmly supporting the new name which then appeared on the publicity for the 1996/97 year. These changes did not alter the essential character of the Training Centre but they were indicative of an ongoing process of formalisation and ongoing development. For example, from the beginning the three stated aims of the course were to produce knowledge, character, and skill in the students. These implicit objectives became codified in straplines that expressed the purpose of Tilsley College.

College Council

Shortly after the Training Centre began a Training Sub-Committee acted as a supervisory body for the training activities and reported back to the Main Committee. The sub-committee included John Speirs as GLO Coordinator, all staff involved on a regular basis and also Graham Hobbs, a Committee Member who had been involved in training in his professional life. In an effort to widen the composition of this group and make consultation more representative, the decision was made to replace the Sub-Committee with the Tilsley College Council. It was important to invite well recognised Christian leaders on to the College Council to add gravitas and raise the college's profile in parts of the country where it was not well known. John Baigent and Ian Burness were asked to join which they willingly did, each serving on the Council for a number of years. The College Council has continued to play an important part in the life of the college and other members over the years have included Paul Young, Jim Crooks, John Wilkes, Esme McFarlane, Ruth Box, Sheila Park, Neil Summerton and Gordon Stewart, who currently is the Chair of the College Council.

A change of administration was planned for 1997, as Ray and Eunice Cawston had decided to leave and return to the mission field, this time in Murcia, Spain where they became part of a Resident GLO Team. Their departure was a huge event for the college as they had shaped and developed training so much and raised standards to the point where the college was

David Clarkson

Stephen McQuoid

now a well-regarded mission training establishment. They had also inspired many groups of students because of their humility and commitment to ministry. A gradual transfer to a new interim team structure took place. Under this structure David Clarkson assumed the role of Principal working alongside Jógvan Zachariassen, who had by this time had joined the staff, Allison Hill and myself. Carolyn Baker also joined the staff on a part time basis to help in the organisation of practical assignments.

David spent the first six months of this tenure on a planned visit to Australia with the staff team continuing in his absence. On his return he focused on team building, but arguably one of the most important initiatives David developed was the Mission Awareness Trip. This consisted of a ten-day expedition at the end of the first module to a location where a GLO Resident Team was operating. The rationale was that the students could be exposed to mission first-hand and a real link could be made between the students and GLO workers in the field.

David was the College Principal for two years and then handed over the role to me, however he continued as a lecturer for some time after this. Jógvan and Unn Zachariassen returned to the Faroes in 1999 so there was the need to look for a new member of staff to join Allison, Carolyn and I.

As the training programme at Tilsley College continued to develop, two distinct priorities were deliberately kept in mind. First, the college existed to train and prepare people specifically for service within GLO. Indeed, on my first day in the job John Speirs told me that success in the job would be judged by how many students joined the work of GLO. Secondly, there was also a desire to train people from an independent church background.

At the heart of GLO

It has always been very difficult to maintain a small training programme in challenging economic conditions and this was certainly the case with Tilsley College. The keys to its survival were its location within a larger campus where a high proportion of overheads were shared between the different ministries of GLO, its location in the Central Belt of Scotland where there is a critical mass of strong churches, its unique selling point of being a college linked with the mission movement that is GLO and that fact that all full-time staff are GLO missionaries and therefore self-supporting. On the other hand, the GLO course had several things in its favour, one of which was its brevity. While a single year of training seemed short and the notion of brevity was unpopular in the wider evangelical world, the quality of candidates proved to be of even greater importance than the length of training. Indeed, some of the most successful missionaries have lacked formal training. Secondly, when a course is short there is a particular need to choose carefully what is taught and how it is taught and consequently the focus is on the basic essentials for service. Moreover on a short course students are made aware of a wide range of resources and viewpoints which they can study further while engaged in Christian service. Arguably this 'on the job' training is the most effective and is focused on real ministry. It should also be noted that the residential component of the one-year GLO course and its intensity make for a truly life changing experience and not one that is merely academically enriching.

Accreditation

As Tilsley College developed more academic sophistication the issue of formal accreditation came to the fore. Once again fears were expressed that the college might become too academic, however it was recognised that rigorous biblical and theological studies have always been at the core of the Christian faith and furthermore educational expectations in society had changed and this needed to be taken into consideration. First some students came to the end of their time at the college and had a desire to go on and do more theological education elsewhere. In order for them to gain credit for what they had studied at Tilsley College the course needed to be formally accredited. Secondly, even students who did not want to do further training nevertheless wanted to have some sort of recognised qualification to show for their efforts. Another consideration was that of visas. It was becoming difficult to obtain study visas for non-EU students and accreditation might help with this. Accreditation also would be good for college staff because an external critique of the college was bound to be more objective and a better point of reference. College staff did not rush into the issue. There was some consultation with Peter Maiden and Pete Williams (now of Tyndale House), both of whom outlined the benefits of accreditation and also the pitfalls of becoming too academically focused.

The arguments in favour of accreditation were compelling, but the work involved was also enormous. Help was at hand, however, in the form of Mark and Shirley Davies, missionaries to Zambia who had a long connection with the GLO work there. Mark joined the college staff and among his first formal tasks was the very daunting pursuit of accreditation which involved dealing with complex systems and a mountain of paperwork. The preferred choice was to go with the European Evangelical Accrediting Association (EEAA), a pan-European body that accredited Bible colleges across Europe, (now known as ECTE). Their systems were robust and the college staff benefitted greatly from their input. By interesting coincidence the head of the EEAA team, that led the accreditation process was Graham Cheesman, my old principal at Belfast Bible College. A second accreditation was later added under the auspices of the British Accreditation Council.

Having gained accreditation it became possible for students to complete the one year Certificate course and then transfer to a degree level course at another institution. Several students have successfully followed this route which in turn has increased the college's standing as an educationally rigorous institution.

Three other initiatives were launched which Mark was also heavily involved with along with most of the staff. First there was the development of a second year Diploma course which took the form of a ministry internship in location with some study weeks back at the college. We had experimented with this idea already through an informal second year course, but it was not until Mark joined the staff that this initiative began to take shape.

Joshua Project

A further development was to recommence evening classes which had actually been run in the past, but never in any systematic way. In 2008 evening classes would begin in earnest and despite some teething problems they have become a significant part of the college's ministry. The development was designed to meet the needs of local churches and enable them to upskill their members. Church leaders were invited to the GLO Centre to talk about the development of future leadership needs. Out of this came a commitment to provide training to meet these needs through an evening class programme that gave a foundation in biblical studies and theology and would also have ministry streams of evangelism, preaching and pastoral care. It was eventually given the name 'Joshua Project' and commenced in Motherwell, and later Stourbridge Dundee, South Wales and London.

Another initiative had international significance. I was concerned that across the world there were many training ministries which were linked with the Brethren movement but had little knowledge of each other. I shared my concerns with college staff as well as with Ian Burness of Echoes of Service and we decided that we would organise a get-together. I had an existing friendship with Ken Daughters of Emmaus Bible College in Dubuque, Iowa in the USA and he offered to host the event completely free of charge. In 2005 some 26 delegates gathered from a dozen countries as far flung as South Korea, India, Zambia and Canada and enjoyed a time of real fellowship and sharing. The consultation not only established good relationships between these training ministries, but the shared experiences and expertise also proved to be very valuable. The Dubuque Consultation, as it has affectionately become known, has been repeated three times (2010, 2014 & 2022) and has grown significantly.

A defining moment in the college's life after so many years of development took place in June of 2010 at the Valedictory Service as I handed over the principalship to Mark Davies. He thus became the fifth principal or leader

Mark Davies

of Tilsley College following in the footsteps of men like Fred Kelling, Ray Cawston and David Clarkson. Mark was to continue the development of the college while Allison and I transferred to the admin department where I took over from John Speirs.

Mark was subsequently succeeded as principal by Simon Marshall who added a third year to the college programme during his tenure. This means that students can study for a one-year Certificate of Higher Education, a two-year Diploma or a three-year European Baccalaureate. During Simon's time as Principal his Academic Dean was Allan McKinnon and when Simon stepped down Allan was asked to become Principal, a position he holds to the present day.

Simon Marshall   Allan McKinnon

Chapter 4

Mission Expands

Once the GLO Centre was firmly established in Motherwell with its training course and short-term missions' programme, it was only going to be a matter of time before more workers from the UK would join their New Zealand and Australian counterparts working cross-culturally. Another unforeseen implication of the establishment of the Motherwell Centre was that those missionaries from Australia and New Zealand would, in due course, come under the umbrella of GLO Europe rather than relate to the GLO Committees back home. This had not been the original plan, but was an example of evolutionary developments on the field.

France

GLO work could now be found in a number of locations beginning with Marseille and Grenoble and then Grasse, Reims and Caen. These early teams were not intended to be church planting, but rather they worked with existing churches, helping them reach out and getting involved in mass literature distribution. The focus on distribution meant that in Marseille for example, the whole city was covered through distribution over a period of several years. There were also potential drawbacks working with existing churches if they did not fully embrace the work of GLO or the missionaries themselves. From a UK perspective the original missionaries, Graham and Alison Black and Margaret Davis were joined by Marian MacIvor and later by Helen Johnston. There was a degree of fluidity as to where these new missionaries went and with whom they would work. For example, Helen Johnston originally was to go to Reims to join Marian, the Emblings and McConnells from New Zealand but went instead to Caen to work alongside the Blacks and Margaret Davis She was to be there for four years before moving on to the work in Marseille.

In Grasse David Goold began building a training centre following pleas from a local Christian. The idea was for the Goolds to live in the Centre along with several trainees and perhaps a national full-time worker. The Centre was built but it did not continue as a Training Centre for a variety of reasons. With several of the missionaries joining on the basis of a two-and-a-half-year commitment it was inevitable that some would move on to other things which is what happened to Margaret Davis and also the Blacks who remain in France as missionaries to this day. Marian MacIvor also served in France for a couple of years, initially in Rheims and then with the Goolds in Grasse before returning to Scotland to help with the bookshop and training ministry at the GLO Centre in Motherwell. Later she joined the work of OM.

Committee grows

Meanwhile back in Motherwell, Geoff and Janet Ruston arrived in 1978, initially to help in the Training Centre. They would soon move from this work into the book ministry and Geoff would also join the GLO Committee in 1980. Two years earlier in 1978 the Committee had been strengthened by the addition of Nelson Logan, David Goold and Graham Hobbs, with Nelson able to represent GLO in Northern Ireland and Graham in the south-west of England. Nelson, an engineer in the defence industry had a long history of involvement in evangelism. As a young man living in Belfast he and some friends including John McQuoid and Reggie Dornan used to take weekends off and cross the border into the Irish Republic to do door-to-door work as well as open-air preaching. In the early 1960s two friends, Arthur Williamson and Bert Gray began Gospel Literature Distribution (GLD), an organisation that recruited young Christians primarily from Northern Ireland to do short-term mission teams in the Republic of Ireland. Nelson, Derek Bingham and a large number of young people got involved and actively reached out to their neighbours south of the border. In 1975 Fred Kelling visited Northern Ireland to recruit team members for the GLO team that was going to Rome as part of the 'Holy Year'. Nelson who had been leading teams to the South, joined the Rome team and found that GLO and GLD were doing the same type of work, so it was decided to merge the two and drop the GLD title.

Further developments

In 1977 Fred and Ruth Kelling joined Nelson to lead a team to Co. Donegal and these Co. Donegal teams continued until 1985 and then later moved to Dublin and then to Navan. It was on one of these Co. Donegal teams that I as a new Christian had my first experience of GLO, one that would shape my life. A significant number of these summer team regulars ended up in full-time Christian service, some of them with GLO.

Following the success of the very first GLO European Workers' Conference in Reims, it was decided to hold an annual event which took place for several years in Devon. These conferences were to prove vital times of fellowship, sharing and planning for the year ahead.

Early GLO Workers' Conference

Back in Australia Colin Tilsley kept a close watch on all of these events and continued to encourage growth not least through the Spearhead magazine to which he contributed regularly . In one edition in 1979 Tilsley stated, 'Wouldn't it be a tremendous thing if every assembly in the so called 'home countries' – Britain, the USA, Canada, New Zealand and Australia were to earnestly ask God to raise up from among them at least one person, or one couple, who could be commended to the overseas mission task in 1979?'

Despite his continued enthusiasm Tilsley's health was rapidly deteriorating and he was spending more and more time in a wheelchair. He wrote about his experiences of suffering in a book entitled 'Through the Furnace' which was advertised in Spearhead and sold through the bookshop. In an effort to encourage him at one of the annual Workers' Conferences in Devon each Committee member recorded a brief message which was then sent to Colin. His death on the 23 March 1981 caused great sadness for all those GLO workers who knew him.

The base in Motherwell continued to grow with Ray and Trixie Keilty becoming house parents at the Training Centre in 1981 and Denise Girling from Southend-on-Sea joining the bookshop and helping in administration. Garry and Connie Engler, a couple from Canada, also joined and helped with practical tasks including printing. The Training Centre was greatly bolstered in 1983 with the arrival of Ray and Eunice Cawston who joined the work initially to be house-parents. Their influence not only shaped the Training Centre, but also GLO as a whole. Eleanor Machray also joined the Book Depot and helped with the accounts.

La Solidarité

Back in France the work continued to enjoy growth and one of the most significant locations that developed greatly was the work in the great Mediterranean city of Marseille. The Goolds were key to this new project having moved back to Marseille from Grasse in 1979 motivated by advice from Brian Tatford who was serving in nearby Aix-en-Provence. They were joined in the work by Helen Johnston, Christine Roy (Swiss), Christine Oliver (Scottish), John McConnell, Brian and Cathy Burgess and Murray and Joy Stevenson (all from New Zealand). The latter couple worked in France for a short time before continuing what would be a lengthy missionary career in Africa. Mark and Anne-Louise Critchlow also joined the team. The work in north Marseille was also to become a church planting work and not just assisting existing churches. This was a deliberate decision which was to some extent shaped by some of the challenges faced by working with existing churches. The initial focus of the work was a large housing development in north Marseille known as La Solidarité. The first group of converts from La Solidarité met in the Goold's house but with the growing numbers they had to find larger accommodation. This was found on the ground floor of a large multi-storey residential block. It was a very tough working-class area that had many social problems. Indeed, so complex were people's lives that the GLO team often had to grapple with difficult issues which felt beyond their depth. Nevertheless they kept going, sharing the gospel and supporting the broken lives of people who came to faith. The work took its toll, however, and Helen Johnston returned home to Belfast exhausted after a decade of challenging work.

Literature continued to be a significant feature of the work and the need arose for a printer in Marseille to provide the tracts. This need was filled in 1982 by Doug and Alison Prescott who, in addition to running a printing press in the same building as the little church in La Solidarité, were also involved in the expansion of the church. This was an exciting development with the printing press producing half million tracts per year to be used by teams all over the country.

Doug Prescott in the Marseille print shop

Les Aygalades

Once the work in La Solidarité became more established the decision was taken to find a new location in which to do some evangelism. This resulted in a small nucleus of Christians who met in an area still in the north of the city called Les Aygalades. Derek and Heather Johnston, along with Christine Roy and Helen Johnston moved from La Solidarité to begin a new work in this area and they were joined by Sam and Andrea Gibson and John and Carol McConnell. Gordon and Hazel Douglas arrived to help the Blacks consolidate the work that had begun in La Solidarité. This church would continue until 1996 when the authorities condemned the building for safety reasons. The Goolds were overseeing the GLO team during all of this period. The small group of believers who met in Les Aygalades never became an established church. Rather it was an outreach point and it was eventually absorbed into La Source, which became the next big project. Significant in this transition were the evangelistic endeavours of Sam Gibson who spent much of his time doing street work and evangelism in the southern suburbs rather than just focusing on Les Aygalades.

La Source

In due course attention focused more on the centre of the city and the planting of the church of La Source (the Source), not far from the city centre and the beautiful Marseille marina. La Source was to grow into a thriving Christian community with a wide variety of activities and outreaches. One key couple who were converted as a result of the work there were Philippe and Marie-Christine Perrilliat who became GLO workers some time later.

The excitement of what was happening in Marseille was passed on to summer team members and it became a very popular summer team destination. More full-time missionaries also came to the city including Paul and Isobel Graham and Ian and Karen Gibson. Both couples were to become heavily involved in evangelism at the university in the south of the city.

Marseille Summer Team

Gordon and Hazel Douglas left Marseille in 1985 and went north to the city of Laval in the Mayenne area to begin church planting there. They were joined by John and Carol McConnell. The following year Mike Packer came to France as a single man but married Alison in September of that year when she joined him in Marseille. By this time the work in La Source had grown sufficiently to allow some of the GLO team to branch out into the south of the city. Sam and Andrea Gibson moved out and were joined by Mike and Alison as well as Marilyn Beer who spent a year with them. From this work a church called Le Rocher (the rock) would come into being. They in turn were joined for a time by Paul and Isobel Graham and Ian and Karen Gibson.

Marseille Resident Team

Moving North

Derek and Heather Johnston moved from Marseille in 1986 and worked in Versailles for a year along with David and Chrissie Young. They linked with Alan and Valerie Kyle who were already missionaries in nearby Rambouillet. The Kyles were a good example of missionaries who had a strong connection with GLO without ever joining. Valerie had been a student on the course in 1977 having spent a couple of months on a short-term GLO team in Caen. Her burden was to go to France as a missionary. Having completed the course she met Alan who was also France bound and they felt they should get married, but not for another year. Valerie then stayed at the GLO Centre in Motherwell to spend that year helping to run the bookshop. Alan and Valerie then went to France, but not with GLO as they felt there was already a large team in Marseille. Instead, their destination was Rambouillet where they settled to serve in the small church. However, they kept in close touch with GLO hosting numerous summer teams over the years.

Back in Marseille

This would not be the end of the changes in Marseille. In the east of the city a new work would emerge resulting in the planting of another church called Le Cep (the vine). Working in this church were three couples, Philippe and Marie-Christine Perrilliat, Graham and Alison Black and Terry and Shona Cobham who had arrived from New Zealand. With the main focus now being concentrated in the south and the east on these new congregations, La Source was left with a lack of strong and mature leadership. This contributed to its eventual closure some years later.

Aubagne

Two significant developments were then initiated. First a relationship was developed with the Geneva Bible Institute in Geneva, a key training establishment for the French-speaking world. This was to be mutually beneficial with a number of GLO workers lecturing at Geneva and Philippe Perrilliat becoming a Board member.

Secondly a new church plant would begin in Aubagne, a town 25km to the east of Marseille which is co-incidentally the headquarters of the French Foreign Legion. Three couples were initially involved in this work, Paul and Isobel Graham, Brian and Hazel Crockett and Sharon Cawston, whose husband Peter continued his medical career in France. After the Crocketts and Cawstons left, Garry and Kim Blair and Daniel and Isabelle Corones (who came to faith through the work at Le Rocher) joined the team. While the Aubagne work was taking place the team fellowshipped in Le Cep and maintained an involvement in the church there, for example Garry was a youth worker in Le Cep. As some people came to faith in Aubagne, services were held there once or twice per month.

Another change occurred after the leaders of Le Rocher and Le Cep felt that they would be helped and strengthened by forming one single congregation in the south of the city. The congregation of Le Rocher moved in with Le Cep which kept its name. A more suitable building was also found for this now larger church. In time the Grahams moved to Scotland to take up a role in pastoral work. Following this it was decided that further consolidation was necessary so the small group in Aubagne was also absorbed into Le Cep.

Laval

Changes were afoot in Laval as well. When Gordon and Hazel Douglas left Laval, John and Carol McConnell continued the work. A significant development happened when they moved the church from their home, where it had been meeting for five years, to a new building. They were able to purchase a place called Le Milk Pub, a non-alcoholic bar and billiard club which became the new home for the church. In time they too left and Mike and Alison Packer went to support the church in that spiritually needy city after some 13 years in Marseille. Their work in Laval was far from easy, not least because Alison developed a long-term health issue. However, their efforts have led to growth in the church in Laval as well as having an impact across the county.

Over a period of several years they pulled together a team to help them reach out to the town of Laval as well as the Mayenne region which is one of the most spiritually needy in the whole of Europe. Catherine King and Sue Gale joined the team and Catherine later married Christian Moreau who was

Mayenne Resident Team 2005

training at Geneva Bible College. Margaret McKay subsequently joined them and when she married Yannick Ollivier the couple continued to help in Laval though eventually moved to the town of Quimper to be involved in ministry there. William and Liz Irwin were also in the team, with Liz having previously worked with OM. Completing the team were Chris and Michelle Hall.

After a number of years working together, the Moreau's and the Halls moved half an hour south to Château-Gontier, a town that did not have any evangelical church so they could engage in pioneer evangelism. Mike and Alison Packer also moved on to pursue ministry in Le Mans. Despite these moves both couples maintain involvement in the church in Laval, with Christian being the pastor and Chris being an elder.

One of the characteristics that distinguished the team in Laval and Château-Gontier over the years was the musical ability of the team members. Consequently, music has played an important part in their ministry. They have conducted summer teams that have had a specific music focus. They have also formed different choirs and singing groups that have held concerts and participated in festivals and a whole variety of gigs.

Music summer team in Laval

GLO Coordinators

Back in the UK the work at the GLO Centre continued to develop. There was need, however, for a strategic decision to be taken with regard to the whole work of GLO. With the death of Colin Tilsley there was the need to clarify the leadership structure of GLO. The three major missionary sending nations were Australia, New Zealand and the UK so representatives from these three met in Sydney to discuss the matter and find a solution. It was agreed that each of these countries should appoint a regional coordinator who would be accountable to their local Committee and could speak on behalf of the work in their jurisdiction. Those leaders were John Speirs for the UK, Roland Forman for New Zealand and Ken Harding for Australia. For John this meant a heavier burden of responsibility at Motherwell and so Joan Schroder joined the work to become the secretary for the Centre at Motherwell and to assist him as PA. Joan came from Folkstone where the Goviers were based. Things developed for Robert Kilpatrick as he went to study at the Bible Training Institute in Glasgow (BTI) and continued to help at the Book Depot and shop whenever he could. Once Robert finished at BTI he took up pastoral ministry in Blandford. John became the Secretary to the GLO Committee with Robert MacPhie doing a stint as GLO Chairman and also helping out with the printing work. There continued to be a great need to promote the work of GLO throughout the UK and in 1985 Jim and Rae Brown joined the work with Jim taking on responsibility to represent the work nationally and later to specifically promote summer teams. David and Anne Hull from Northern Ireland also joined the work to promote mission there.

It was at this time that a much-needed refurbishment of the Centre took place. The church building at the heart of the complex was built to an unusual Byzantian style mimicking the Hagia Sophia in Istanbul. Consequently, it was a listed property and so there were strict limitations on what could be done with the building. An extensive redecoration produced an auditorium which downstairs could seat 200 with a further 300 seats in the balcony. The area beneath the balcony was partitioned off to be used for additional workspace. Some of it was used to extend the bookshop so as to enable an increase in its stock capacity. Another area was used for the coffee shop which continued to be run by Cathie Speirs. The remainder of this area was used for offices, including office space for John Speirs and Joan Schroder. All of this increased the business aspect of the Centre which, with the addition of the book distribution work throughout Scotland and North-East England, made the GLO Centre an important Christian resource centre for the west of Scotland.

Wider relations

As the physical layout of the Motherwell Centre changed so too did the relationships with our sister organisations, Echoes of Service and the Home and Foreign Mission Fund (which then became Interlink prior to its amalgamation with Echoes). Up until 1991 GLO workers were not included in the Echoes Daily Prayer Guide and there was no formal agreement between the two organisations. Perhaps this was unsurprising as GLO was the 'new kid on the block' and it had a very different working culture to the other two groups. The change, however, was good news and progress was made.

The change began as early as June of 1989 when WK Morrison was invited to a meeting at the Central Hotel in Glasgow for an informal chat with Peter Grosvenor and David Restall of Echoes and Willie McInnes of Home and Foreign Mission Fund.

This was followed by another meeting in January of 1990, this time between GLO and Echoes to exchange views and explore any commonalities. This became a regular occurrence between GLO and Echoes with Home and Foreign joining at particular interludes. As the organisations got to know each other and appreciate each other's strengths, an agreement was reached as to how to work together. The agreement which was announced in March of 1991 was that any GLO worker commended from an independent church in the UK and serving overseas would be included in the Echoes Daily Prayer Guide which meant that they would enjoy the same support and benefits as every other missionary associated with Echoes. With this first step in place it was only a short time later that Home and Foreign Mission Fund, which operated exclusively in Scotland, afforded GLO workers the same privileges. The impact of this decision was a unity of purpose between the three organisations and an ongoing cooperation in mission.

Recruitment

With the work in France taking shape it was important to begin something substantial in Italy as well. From 1982 onwards adverts began to appear in Spearhead asking for prospective missionaries to go to Italy. In 1984 an Italian couple by the name of Tom and Anna D'Andrea joined the work in Italy and began organising summer teams in several locations around the country.

By this stage many of the summer team members and full-time GLO workers were coming from Northern Ireland and so it was seen as an important resource country for team recruitment. The initiative was taken to begin annual weekends in Castlewellan Castle so that team members and potential team members could hear Bible teaching, enjoy fellowship and gain some more experience in evangelism. At their height these weekends were attended by over a hundred young people. A small committee including Nelson Logan, Garry Jebb, Elspeth Mackie, Alan and David Wilson and Gavin McQuoid was established to run the weekend and to convene monthly mission prayer meetings in Nelson's home as well as conducting a GLO roadshow around churches. These events produced much fruit although the Committee was disbanded some years later.

The importance of residential weekends could also be seen in Scotland where an annual Reunion was held in the autumn for summer team members. These were memorable events where every bit of floor space was utilised for sleeping and eating arrangements and where speakers would challenge those who came along to commit to mission.

GLO Centre extension

With the work still growing, the time came again for more refurbishment work at the Centre. This was to take place in 1985 (see chapter 3). Second hand school classroom units were obtained from a local school and reassembled to create study bedrooms for the Training Centre as well as a new lounge, lecture room and committee room. Included in the work would be a general clean-up of the site making the Centre more attractive. At the heart of this project was the laying of paving across much of the site which became an enormous benefit as the Centre used to get very muddy particularly in the winter. The layout of the Centre also changed as the council gave permission for the Muir Street entrance to be closed off and a new entrance opened up at Pollock Street. This also meant the Centre was slightly extended with land given by the council. Because of the Scottish Development Agencies' involvement, GLO only had to pay 10% of the overall cost of the project. It was a significant job which involved laying 66,000 bricks and erecting 100 sheets of plasterboard. The work was made possible by the efforts of local Christians who volunteered to help. With all this work invested in the Centre it became apparent that it would be much better for GLO to become the owner and not just continue to lease the premises from the Church of Scotland. Meetings were set up with the leadership of the Church and the proposal was put to them. Their response was not particularly swift and over a four-year period these meetings continued on a six-monthly basis. However, the Church finally agreed with our proposal and so GLO bought the whole property in 1989 for the princely sum of £90,000.

Building extension work

With the physical structure of the GLO Centre taking shape it was impor-tant to apply some thought to the organisational infrastructure of GLO. Up until this point there was little by way of defined roles or teams nor how they should relate to each other. Ray Cawston wrote a paper called 'Looking Ahead' which made some proposals for restructuring life at the Centre. This paper was discussed and in February and March some changes were implemented. Also the bookshop and training personnel were put into teams so that there was more clarity as to who worked where and the demarcation of responsibilities.

What was true of changing life in the Centre also became true of the work as a whole. At the Workers' Conference of 1985 there was substantial discussion about how GLO as a whole should be organised and also about the relationship between GLO and local churches. This led to a policy statement being produced the following year based on those discussions. The policy statement, which was circulated to the entire work, laid out GLO's doctrinal statement, some practical issues including GLO Centre administration and training and also a diagram that articulated the overall structure of GLO. This structure included the Main Committee as well as sub-committees for Mission Teams, Training, Finance, and Coordination. It also included teams in the Motherwell Centre such as the Training team, coordination of evangelism, coffee shop, wholesale books, retail books, youth ministries, not forgetting a team at the Kirkcaldy Centre. On the field, the new structure included French teams in Marseille, Versailles, Laval and also in Spain, a team in Galicia consisting of missionaries from New Zealand. The Mission sub-committee also reflected on how new mission situations should come into being. It was agreed that if a missionary wanted to go into a new area, they were required to draw up a paper researching the area, its spiritual needs and the existing evangelical witness there. Then this paper was to be submitted to the Mission sub-committee for approval. GLO was coming of age and beginning to get organised.

Chapter 5

Growing the Book Ministry

When Robert Kilpatrick started the book ministry, the challenge was always going to be how to maintain and expand it. This was particularly important when Robert went to study at BTI before moving on to church ministry in Blandford. Around the same time Marian MacIvor who was also involved in the book ministry left to join OM. Initially this gap filled by Valerie Conroy (later to become Kyle) whose background was radiography, so book ministry was totally new to her and a daunting challenge. Valerie recalls an occasion when she was ordering books from a rep who asked her, 'do you realise how much money you are spending?' after which the sympathetic rep reduced the size of the order.

It was to the book ministry that Geoff and Janet Ruston would commit themselves some time after their arrival in Motherwell in January 1978. Geoff had been a bank official and Janet a nurse. Working with books was not their first role; they came to be house parents for the students with Janet doing the cooking and washing as well as some secretarial work. Fred Kelling who was acting as GLO Treasurer also involved Geoff in some of the book-keeping.

Initially Geoff and Janet relieved some of the work pressure in the bookshop by helping Valerie with the bookkeeping. Then when Valerie left to go to France as a missionary, Joyce Halsall, who had served in Tanzania, was asked to take over the bookshop but preferred instead to take on Janet's role. Janet was then approached and agreed to be Valerie's replacement, requiring a very fast learning curve as she had no experience in retail either.

Geoff & Janet Ruston

Beginning with basics

The early days of the book ministry were very rudimentary. The bookshop that Robert Kilpatrick opened in Hamilton with the help of volunteers was transferred to the GLO Centre in Motherwell shortly after the property had been acquired by GLO. While this was an improvement, the GLO Centre was itself fairly basic, initially consisting of an unused church building with many of its windows still boarded up, an old church hall and a large wooden hut. The bookshop, once in Motherwell, occupied a space in the foyer of the church building. As the church building was gradually refurbished, offices were built under what was the balcony of the church building. Much of the refurbishment over the years would be done by an army of volunteers such as David Peat who also was a regular on summer teams. The centre of the auditorium floor, however, was still filled with old pews and other debris as a leftover remnant of its previous abandonment. The turnover in the bookshop in those early days was £20,000, a significant achievement, but nothing compared to what would develop over the next couple of decades.

Original Bookshop at the GLO Centre

Wholesale

STL, the book distribution division of OM which operated from a large warehouse in Bromley, had been a major supplier to the bookshop from the start. Their small storage facility in Glasgow was not sufficient to re-stock the Bookmobile when it came up periodically from Kent so GLO was approached to take this on and develop it. This was agreed and a space was cleared in the centre of the church building for this to happen and GLO was given an old Walls sausage van to facilitate this. A useful spin-off from this clearance was that some of the old pews were sold while others were used to repair the leaking roof of the church building. Robert Kilpatrick initiated this work and Geoff took it on 18 months after arriving at GLO. This division of labour with Janet focusing her energies on the bookshop while Geoff focused on the wholesale business was to occupy the couple for many years.

From these exciting and adventurous early days, both the bookshop and the Book Depot ministry continued to grow. Whenever possible restructuring was done at the Centre so as to develop the ministry and improve things. With this in mind a refurbishment of the church building was carried out in 1981 and a small coffee shop was opened just beside the bookshop utilising space under the balcony of the church. This added considerably to the attraction of the bookshop and indeed the Centre as a whole and typical of these early days in GLO the coffee shop was dependent on volunteers for it to function.

Geoff Ruston with book van

Sales grow

Two years later it was becoming clear that the space in the church building was not adequate for housing the wholesale book depot ministry so the old wooden Boys Brigade hut that lay in the grounds was cleared out and everything moved there. Even this was not an ideal location - the hut was stiflingly hot in the summer and freezing cold in the winter. It did however offer suitable space and the wholesale business grew and grew. Sales were divided between goods ordered from the depot which were posted out and goods sold by Geoff as he travelled around Scotland and the north of England. It meant that he had a whole network of Christians that he kept in touch with, often enjoying their hospitality while on his travels. In 1980 van sales were £80,569 while the depot cleared £48,151 worth of stock leading to a grand total of £128,720. By 1983 van sales accounted for £107,157 and depot sales were £90,054. These very healthy sales peaked in 1987 with van sales of £176,630 and depot sales of £248,331 making a grand total for that year of £424,961. What had begun as a simple ministry to serve churches turned out also to be a great income generating mechanism for GLO. What is more the contacts and goodwill that Geoff built up by travelling around the country were equally valuable.

Boys' Brigade hut

The rapid growth of the depot ministry meant that the old BB hut became too small, let alone being inadequate as a place to work. When a significant refurbishment of the Centre took place in 1985, one section of the extension became the new Book Depot and the old BB hut was knocked down to make way for the new development.

Several staff supported Geoff in the book depot and made vital contributions, including Eleanor Machray who took responsibility for much of the admin. Visitors to the depot had memories of Eleanor, keeping warm by a gas fire, trying to keep the books in order. Several volunteers also offered great service, among them Bill Galloway and Tom McNeish who gave two days and four days a week respectively for a great many years. Towards the end of the book depot ministry Annette Campbell joined the staff before transferring to the bookshop where she still works.

Book Depot staff

The book depot ministry continued until 1989 when the Bromley and Motherwell depots were consolidated within STL's huge new facility in Carlisle. It was the end of an era and a ministry that had provided a great deal of much needed finance for GLO as well as establishing goodwill and many contacts throughout Scotland and the north of England. Over this time the wholesale ministry had serviced 129 shops, 83 of them serviced by the van as

Geoff travelled more than 20,000 miles in 60 trips annually. More than 1200 parcels were also sent out direct from the depot each year. All of this made it a worthwhile venture and an important part of GLO history. This did not mean the end of Geoff's ministry. During this time he had become GLO Treasurer and this developed into the GLO Business Ministries manager, a role which would also include responsibility for the running of the Kirkcaldy Centre.

The bookshop was also to experience significant growth under Janet's leadership, and like the depot, those who worked in the bookshop did not see it merely as a business that generated income - it was a ministry that helped the Church and supported mission. This affected the whole ethos of the shop. Staff saw themselves as being there to help Christians and to offer a service to the wider public. It was not unusual for advice on books to turn into a spiritual conversation in which the staff member would encourage a Christian to go on in their faith or encourage a non-Christian to read the Bible, attend church or simply think about deeper spiritual realities. On one occasion, for example, a woman came into the shop and asked for a Bible. Marion Mathers was at the counter and asked if the Bible was for herself and if she wanted a modern version. The woman responded by saying that she had cancer which was at an advanced stage and she only had a matter of weeks to live. She said 'I don't know if I have left it too late to start reading the Bible'. Marion assured her it was never too late and sold the woman the Bible. This is just one of many such incidents where Christian love and help was given.

It was a great blessing that the GLO complex included the coffee shop because combined with bookshop and auditorium, the GLO Centre became a meeting place for Christians. I can remember arriving to work at GLO in 1990 and for my first couple of years joined Roman Road Hall where I had been as a student. On Saturday mornings some of the men at church played football and the post-match routine was to head back to the GLO Coffee Shop for breakfast followed by a browse around the bookshop looking for Christian albums or any new stock. It was also a place of mercy. The socio-economic conditions that prevailed in Motherwell in the 80s and 90s in the aftermath of the closure of the Ravenscraig steel plant meant that unemployment, deprivation and homelessness were common. Bookshop staff along with their coffee shop counterparts became very familiar with homeless people who often frequented the Centre and while there was little practical help that could be offered other than a sandwich, a mug of tea, Christian guidance and witness, this was gladly offered.

Factors for growth

Firstly, up to 1989 the close proximity of the wholesale depot meant that there was always 'back up stock' readily available and so what was an initially modest bookshop was actually a great resource. Now the space vacated by the depot was available for the bookshop to move from the church and undergo a major refit. Secondly the bookshop had built up a large and dedicated group of book agents who ran bookstalls in their local churches. This not only meant that more books were being sold but also that the bookshop was being publicised over a wide area. These book agents were often motivated, not just by their interest in Christian books and the value that they saw in them, but also out of a desire to help the work of GLO. The two things came together and the bookshop was known to all as the GLO Bookshop.

A third factor for growth was the renovations that helped every department within GLO. The renovation of the church building in 1981 meant a refurbishment of the bookshop, a new coffee shop and the availability of a large auditorium, all of which drew attention to the Centre and brought more people to it. The ethos of the bookshop was also important. With this being primarily a ministry, both Geoff and Janet wanted to ensure that the quality of books remained high. Study books and commentaries were expensive and sold slowly therefore tying up a lot of capital on the shelves for prolonged periods of time. However, while stocking lots of these high-end items made little economic sense, it did make a great deal of sense from a ministry point of view. Material that Geoff referred to as 'holy haberdashery' (pencils, bookmarks and even Christian jewellery) sold well but they did not want them to take over the whole shop so a careful balance was maintained. Consequently the bookshop built a reputation for being a primary seller of Bibles, theology books and teaching resources.

Perhaps the most important secret of success was the team that ran the bookshop. This included not only the full-time and part-time salaried members of staff, but also the GLO staff workers and the army of volunteers. It was more than just a job; the bookshop team saw themselves as serving God by utilising the medium of the written word.

The growth of the bookshop over the years could tangibly be seen in retail figures. In 1975 the shop carried stock worth £2,780 and had sales for the year of £12,080. By 1981 the amount of stock had risen to £61,480 with sales of £198,214. At the peak there were 75 book agents and sales through them exceeded £40,000. Today in a very different era and at a time when the vast majority of Christian bookshops across the United Kingdom have closed, we are grateful not only to be still open, but sales for 2023 are in excess of £250,000. Long-term staff such as Marion Mathers (who was the first person employed by the bookshop), Annette Campbell, Helen Dempsey and Andrew Lacey along with full-time workers such as Kathleen Boyden (later to become Kathleen McFadden) and Grace Goulding, provided a stability that enabled a consistent service over the years. Their work was greatly helped over the years by the many dedicated volunteers (too many to mention) who came to help in whatever way they could.

1992 was a memorable year for two reasons. Negatively, it was the year that a fire caused massive damage to the church building. While this did not directly affect the bookshop as it had already moved to the extension, all the ministries in the GLO Centre were in some way adversely affected. The other event was much more positive - the computerisation of the bookshop. This did prove a challenge to some of the volunteers who decided they did not have the skill set or computer knowledge to keep helping out, however it did lead to a more efficient way of running the shop. Computerisation would also eventually become universal throughout the Centre and made doing business in GLO as a whole more efficient and cost effective.

New management

Towards the end of the nineties things were changing again. Janet, along with running a busy bookshop, was also involved with other ancillary ministries, including an Emmaus correspondence ministry with the help of Garry Engler (who was caretaker for some years) and George Watson. For health reasons, she felt the need to have a reduced role so in 1997 she took over the day to day running of the general GLO finances and Geoff took over the running of the bookshop handing over his Business Ministries responsibilities to Ian Smith. Ian and his wife Jenny had recently joined the work of GLO and this change effectively made Ian Geoff and Janet's new boss. It was in this spirit of teamwork and mutual accountability that the GLO Business Ministries were run.

Sales continued to be strong despite the competition from other suppliers which was now being felt. In an effort to keep up with the demands of modern retailing in the year 2000 there was a reconfiguration of the extension, and the bookshop was given 30% more retail space and a substantial revamp and face lift. This, along with the many years of hard work that had gone on before, bore fruit in another way. In 2002 the GLO Bookshop won the prestigious UK 'Large Christian Retailer of the Year' award at the Christian Booksellers Convention, an award it would win again. Considering the humble origins of the ministry - an empty chip shop in Hamilton followed by the move to a disused church in Motherwell. This was a significant milestone. Sales had also climbed just above the £400,000 mark (a personal ambition for Geoff) and this was generating much needed funding for the work of GLO.

Ian Smith

Changing hands again

In 2003 Geoff and Janet felt that they would like to initiate a new ministry supplying books to the majority world. Overseas Publishing and Literature Trust (OPAL) as it was called was formed along with John Lewis who had also been involved with GLO in the launching of the Kirkcaldy Centre. With Geoff leaving the work a new bookshop manager was needed – enter Andrew Lacey.

Andrew had been the manager of a large supermarket in Strathaven but was looking for an opportunity to serve God within a Christian organisation. His appointment brought about a significant change because while Geoff and Janet had been full-time GLO workers, Andrew came on board as a salaried employee, albeit significantly below the normal commercial level. Strathaven Evangelical Church where Andrew was an Elder at the time, was very supportive of the move and this was seen by all as a ministry position not just another job.

Things were changing in the Christian book market at this time and so the challenge for the staff in trying to maintain the bookshop was going to be immense. The internet was revolutionising retailing and books were among the first commodities to be sold heavily in this way. This was coupled with a general decline in reading among Christians and the advent of the e-book and e-readers meant that physical books had a great deal of competition, especially among digital natives.

Andrew Lacey

Christian bookshops across the country began to close because they could not maintain profitability. This challenge also affected general book-shops with some very large high street names going under. Supply also became a major problem as some of the biggest distributors of Christian books in the UK went out of business, sometimes leaving behind substantial debts. Working against the trend the GLO Bookshop continued doing business even though both margins and profits were substantially lower. The wining of the 'Large Christian Retailer of the Year' award for the second time in 2010 was a real encouragement as well as a wonderful achievement given the difficult climate in which it was operating. Sadly between 2000 and the present day well over half of all Christian book-shops in the UK have closed. Indeed, of those that keep operating, many are small and rely on volunteers or the benevolence of a church that sees the bookshop as part of its own ministry. It is in this context that the GLO

Bookshop staff

Bookshop had to operate and continues to make a positive contribution to GLO income.

Times have changed as the bookshop now puts less money back into GLO than in the past. However, the ministry ideals remain the same and there is a continued determination to serve the church and the community by supplying good quality resources. The bookshop team works hard by innovating and offering increased services. A website offers internet sales, and the opening of a second-hand section has been a significant addition to the shop. E-books are now available through the bookshop and it also hosts events based around book evenings which profile authors and ministries. Book reviews are also sent out regularly to hundreds of Christian leaders in several countries and the shop is willing to supply their book needs at reasonable cone. All of this is because we have the conviction that our book ministry is not just about making a profit, but we are in the business of mission and everyone linked with the bookshop is intentional about making their contribution.

The combination of the bookshop, coffee shop and the conferencing facilities has made the GLO Centre an important facility for churches and Christian

Current bookshop

organisations as well as the general public. Indeed, so central to the community has the bookshop and Centre become that local schools now use the bookshop as a placement for school children who are doing work experience. The Centre continues to live up to the 'tag-line' that Geoff Ruston created many years ago – 'Scotland's Leading Independent Christian Resource Centre'.

Chapter 6

Up in Smoke

In the late 80s and early 90s my parents were living in the North East of England. I was visiting them on the Christmas of 1992 when I received a dramatic phone call from Ray Cawston. Ray and Eunice at the time were living in the upper flat of the manse at the GLO Centre with Geoff and Janet Ruston living downstairs. Ray's phone message that Boxing Day was short and startling. 'Don't be alarmed and don't cut short your Christmas break', he said, 'I just thought you should know that there has been a fire and the church building has been destroyed'.

My concern, not to mention curiosity, meant I could not stay away any longer, so I immediately drove back to Motherwell to see what had happened. The scene that greeted me on my arrival back at GLO was horrendous. From the outside the church building looked no different, though the smell of smoke and charred wood was still pungent even while standing outside in the fresh air. Entering the building, however, the smell became so overpowering it made my eyes water and the visible evidence of the fire was immediately apparent. An investigation would later reveal that someone had set fire to a milk crate outside the building next to an air vent and the flames were sucked through the vent and under the floor of the church building.

The inferno

The damage caused by the fire was extensive. The floor area of the auditorium was badly burned to the point where a substantial section of flooring was no longer there. Most of what remained were the charred remains of the timbers that had supported the floor. All the wiring and pipework that had previously been hidden under the floor was now exposed and damaged. The old church organ which had stood in that site since the building was first constructed was also destroyed. The smoke from the fire had marked most of the walls and large sections of the balcony had burned away making it unsafe to go up there. Any equipment in the building was destroyed and virtually nothing could be salvaged from the coffee shop. The brass chandeliers were badly tarnished and the heat had been so intense that one of the stone pillars holding up the roof of the building had started to crumble. This beautiful building which not only gave the Centre its character and was also a hub of activity, was now utterly unusable and in need of massive restoration.

Fire damage

What became very obvious was that the building either needed major work, or it needed to be abandoned altogether. That stark reality did not make the decision making any easier. The enormity of the building and repair work that would be required would have a high price tag attached to it. The facilities the building offered were very important to the proper functioning of GLO, but spending big money when you are a missionary organisation supporting missionaries who are themselves often struggling just to make ends meet, is a decision fraught with complication. Big questions would be asked about GLO's priorities. Accusations could be made that GLO was more interested in maintaining a substantial HQ rather than supporting workers on the front line. After all what was GLO really about, preaching to the lost or maintaining buildings?

The weight of this decision lay heavily on the shoulders of the GLO Main Committee with members of the Committee being pulled in different directions. This was not a decision that could be taken lightly or quickly. That said, the absence of the facilities that the church building provided was very disruptive to life at the Centre and greatly complicated work practices, so a decision had to be arrived at quickly. While the bookshop had previously moved to the new building, the coffee shop and some offices had remained in the church building. Consequently, the coffee shop had to cease operations and the staff who worked in the church building had to find makeshift offices elsewhere. The auditorium was frequently used for meetings and events - all of this came to an end. It was also where the annual student Valedictory Service took place and so in the June of 1993, with no auditorium available for use, it was held in the much more cramped church halls.

The big decision

A Building Survey and Feasibility Study were carried out to ascertain what could be done to repair the damage. It became clear there were two options to consider. First, the church building could be restored to its previous condition - a large auditorium with a balcony. This was a more limited option because it would mean that when the coffee shop was operating nothing else could take place in the building at the same time. Any events scheduled for the auditorium could only happen when the coffee shop was shut and the space transformed from a coffee shop to a meeting room. Of course this was how it had already been, but the question now was whether this situation could be improved upon. This led to a second option being considered which would inevitably be more expensive. The second possibility was for a new floor to be built at the base of the balcony, effectively converting the church into a two-storey building. This would mean that the upstairs section would become the auditorium and could hold separate events at the same time the coffee shop operated downstairs. There would be no need to change the coffee shop around every time an event took place and the same building could be used to do much more.

An architect was employed to prepare detailed plans and tenders were issued so that costings could be made. The total cost for the rebuilding work was £391,000. The figure was huge, however there was some help in the form of an insurance payment. The offer made by the insurance company in light of the damage caused by the fire was £193,562 for the building plus £9,560 for contents. This meant that GLO would have to raise around £188,000 in order to make this a possibility, a big ask back in 1993!

The Main Committee had to make a decision but there was unlikely to be unanimity. Given the significance of the decision it was also agreed that GLO workers should be informed about the plans and be able to contribute to the final proposal. After a great deal of prayer and deliberation it was decided to go ahead with the two-storey option.

The whole process took around a year and a half before the building work was complete. One encouragement was that people in the community wrote to express their sadness at the closure of the coffee shop and their desire to see it reopen again. Once the decision was made to go ahead, the serious business of fundraising began. Given the church background of most GLO workers, asking directly for money was definitely not part of the GLO psyche. This, however, was a special case and the Committee felt that it would be important to be honest and transparent with the wider Christian public about the needs of GLO. A special publicity brochure was published for circulation which tackled the issue head on. It contained a description of the ministries that could take place in the new building including a coffee shop, youth and children's ministries, a pottery to help unemployed young people as well as the facility of a permanent and modern auditorium seating 300. This could be available to be used by GLO Extension Ministries as well as other Christian organisations. The brochure included the architect's drawings of what the finished building would look like as well as the costs involved in the whole project.

Generous donations

Moved by this appeal, churches and individual Christians began to respond. By the time of the spring edition of Spearhead 1994 over £60,000 had been donated and by the time tax was reclaimed this amount had risen to over £70,000. However, that still left more than £100,000 to be raised. The job was both huge and time consuming. In addition to replacing the downstairs floor, balcony and inserting a new cantilever floor for the upstairs auditorium, the internal stone cleaning had to be done as well as replacing the damaged masonry from the pillars.

By the summer of 1994 the work was finished and on 24th June over 1000 visitors came to the opening day to view the revitalised building. All income from donations and the insurance claim had amounted to £320,000 requiring only £80,000 to be borrowed to complete the project. Two Christian trusts had made loans at a very favourable rate which eased the pressure significantly.

It was not long before the building was full of activity again and has been well used ever since. The rightness of the decision to spend to money and upgrade the facilities has been well vindicated. Indeed even now, the hiring of the facilities and in particular the hiring of the auditorium and coffee shop space is one of the most important generators of finance for GLO today.

Auditorium

In later years, someone who did a great deal to develop the conferencing ministry was Anna McRobert (née Pinney) who joined the work after studying at Tilsley College and then worked both in Kirkcaldy and Motherwell Centres. Her specific role in Motherwell was to publicise and administer the conferencing facilities and to work alongside Angela Rendall, the coffee shop manager. The auditorium is now widely recognised as an excellent meeting room. It has been used by churches and a whole variety of groups from schools to the local music society. The Scottish Court Service has also hired the facility on three separate occasions for Public Enquiries. It has helped make the GLO Centre one of the most significant resources available to the local community and local churches. In large measure the bookshop and coffee shop have put GLO on the map locally and enable the ministry of GLO to be appreciated by people in the area.

One of the uses of the auditorium was the annual Mini Bible School which has been running for over 20 years. In the early days most of the speakers were GLO workers who brought teaching on relevant subjects and offered a biblical perspective. More recently we have utilised more guest speakers and also broadened the subject areas, but still maintaining our aim to provide relevant biblical teaching on contemporary issues.

While so much focus had to be given to dealing with the GLO Centre fire and its effects, of necessity, life for GLO continued very much as normal. Away from buildings and plans there was the ongoing need to continue attracting young people to mission. An initiative was launched in conjunction with Echoes of Service called the Youth Strategy Group. I was given the job of leading this along with Ian Burness and a team of volunteers including Martin Erwin, Chrissie Hayman, Paul Knox, Dave Young, May Barr and later Allison Hill who first joined as a minute taker. The YSG only ran for a few years but in that time it convened numerous youth mission events across the country, began a youth magazine called Planet View and produced a World Mission Resource Pack which helped youth leaders introduce the subject of mission to their youth groups, along with a second one aimed at children. A highlight for the YSG was an apologetics training weekend that was held at Scargill House in Yorkshire at which the guest speakers were Philip Johnston, John Lennox and the late Professor David Gooding.

On the field

Meanwhile a new work began in Romania. Mervyn and Liz Symons had come over to Romania under the auspices of GLO Australia and settled in Talmaciu in central Romania where a new GLO Centre opened. The work there was varied. First there was Bible teaching as the GLO missionaries helped the already established Golgota Bible School which was run by local believers. Then a printing work developed which was initially run by an Australian missionary couple, Heiko and Alison Reicken. Complementing this work was an English teaching ministry run by a couple of young missionaries Lorelle Moase and Natalie Pocock, again both from Australia. Finally, a kindergarten ministry was begun in the Talmaciu Centre. This Australian and New Zealand team would eventually be replaced by two Romanian couples, George and Lidia Sortan and Dani and Doina Vasilca who would in turn come under the auspices of GLO Europe as a natural evolution of the work. Dani and Doina would be involved in a range of children's ministries while George and Lidia were involved in church planting and church support among the gypsy community.

Radio ministry

In time, George and Lidia's son Cristi would come to Tilsley College to study and then return to Romania to join the ministry. Now married to

Simone, he runs a youth and children's ministry linked to the gypsy work and disciples young Christians. Dani and Doina's children's ministry also greatly expanded as they began to produce and broadcast online children's programmes and Sunday schools. These proved a particular blessing during the Covid pandemic and they reach children not only in Romania itself, but children that are part of the Romanian diaspora all over Europe.

The Closure of Kirkcaldy

The issue of property and the complications linked with it were often the subject of Committee Meetings. While the Motherwell Centre continued to play a very central part in the life and organisation of GLO, the same could not be said for the centre in Kirkcaldy. For much of its existence it proved a great blessing in the town and it also managed to be self-sustaining even though the coffee shop tended to make more money than the bookshop. The Main Committee had often reflected on whether GLO should open more bookshops. Certainly the Motherwell bookshop in particular had brought in a significant amount of funding over the years and some Committee members wondered if other bookshops could do the same. Indeed there was even talk of taking over an empty property in Largs and opening a Christian bookshop there. In the end this was decided against. Geoff had been keeping a careful eye on the book trade and believed that it would become increasingly difficult for Christian bookshops to remain profitable. Given recent history this has proved to be a wise decision.

The issue at hand, was what to do with the Kirkcaldy Centre. The reason this issue arose was because it ceased to be profitable and it was becoming increasingly difficult to find volunteers to staff it. The decision was made more difficult because the Centre had been such a blessing and there were many Christians in the town, and indeed the whole area who put a high value on its work. In the end a local businessman approached GLO with the proposal that he would purchase the Centre from GLO and use it as an outreach centre for the town. The Main Committee agreed and in 2004 the GLO Centre in Kirkcaldy closed its doors for the last time which brought to an end an important component in the history of GLO.

Chapter 7

Generation Next

Nothing stands still! One of the realities of life is that things change. As the 1980s came to a close for GLO the work developed and matured and with this came changes. On 30th September 1988 one of the very first GLO workers, David Prosser, passed away after battling for some time with a brain tumour. It was a sad but not unexpected event. There were other evidences of change within the work. Some of the first generation of missionaries had either retired from Christian work or had gone on to other ministries or organisations. In several of the locations where Resident Teams had operated the missionaries had now moved on. The work was long enough in the making for some of the churches that had been helped to now be standing on their own two feet. However, the challenges in secular Europe being what they are, some others had closed their doors.

Viewpark

Up until this point much of the focus of missionary work had been in France and perhaps not surprisingly, as the needs there were so acute. However, there were other new initiatives emerging - one just a few miles from the GLO Centre in Motherwell. It was a new church planting project in the housing estate of Viewpark. With a concentrated population of 8,500 people the area of Viewpark on the outskirts of Glasgow had been designated an area of 'Priority Treatment' by the local Council. It had been estimated that less than 1% of British working-class people attended church and most lived in areas like Viewpark with high unemployment, single parent families and the twin problems of drug and alcohol abuse.

Viewpark housing estate

The team that began the work in Viewpark consisted of David and Sheena Buchan, Colin MacPhie (soon to be married to Margaret) and Lorna Paterson. David had come from a social work background and his skills and experience would be well used in this church planting venture. In the early days the team were supported and encouraged by the nearby Bothwell Evangelical Church (now Grace Church, Bothwell). The team lived on the estate and tried to find practical ways of addressing some of the felt needs which included children's and youth work in local schools. An elderly couple who were long-term residents on the estate, David and Jean Wood and Jean's sister Betty were already running a small Sunday School in their home and they welcomed the GLO team to help. This gave them immediate inroads into the community. Steve Ellacott from Bothwell Evangelical Church also supported the work from the earliest days. The team obtained a council house on the estate which was used as a base and after a few converts began to attend, Sunday services started and they then moved into a community centre located in the centre of the estate. The new church was named the Viewpark Christian Fellowship.

In 1992 Debbie Williams (later to become McQuoid) joined the team and was particularly involved in youth and women's ministries.

Viewpark Resident Team 1996

As the work developed and converts matured, Lorna moved on and David and Sheena also felt free to leave Viewpark and to join a new team headed up by Pierre and Alison Bariteau in Bagnols-sur-Cèz in the south of France. This meant that the MacPhies and Debbie remained on the team and were joined for a while by Joanna Brind (who later to become Baxter). The fledgling church was helped by a young couple from Bothwell, Alan and Margaret Brodie, who joined while maintaining their existing jobs. A landmark for the church occurred when John Dick, who had become a Christian as a result of the work, studied at Tilsley College before going on to work in Cardiff with Thornhill Church and subsequently joined the team in Johnstone as a GLO worker. Today John is pastor at Craighalbert Church near Glasgow.

A further development followed in 2005 with a change in location for the church. For some time attempts were made to find a permanent building somewhere in the Viewpark area. None of these proved successful and it was becoming increasingly awkward operating out of the local community centre. A couple of miles down the road in the neighbouring town of Bellshill, a small group of believers in what was then Orbiston Gospel Hall were praying for someone to take over their church building as they planned to merge with another nearby church. Their building was in the middle of the Orbiston estate which was a very similar area to Viewpark. After an initial meeting between the two groups of Elders in the autumn of 2004, it was agreed that the members of the Gospel Hall would sell their building to the Viewpark Christian Fellowship for a modest sum. The building was in need of substantial renovation but was ideally located to reach into the community of Orbiston. Now that the church had moved out of Viewpark a change of name was necessary. The name was changed to Liberty Community Church. For a short time Al and Lynsey Burt worked part time with the church. Now Liberty Community Church is fully established and operating with its own leadership structure and without a GLO Resident Team.

Italy

Expansion was happening elsewhere too. In August 1988, Robert and Muriel Hamilton along with their three young children (5, 4 and 3) came from Newtownards to Motherwell to do the one-year GLO 'Training for Service' course with a view to going to Italy as part of a GLO Resident Team the following year. One year later with an extra two kids in-tow (twins Philip and Steven born in Motherwell), they found themselves in the university city of Perugia, studying Italian. Studying language three months at a time and taking turns to look after the children, they felt far from fluent we they moved to the huge city of Naples to work alongside the inner-city church at Fuorigrotta in January 1991. They had committed for one year with the possibility of staying for a further three if things went well. In the end they stayed 17 years in what is one of Europe's most chaotic yet charming cities.

Dealing with the language was not easy, not least because Neapolitan is hugely different from classic Italian. Furthermore, there were many internal conflicts and struggles in the leadership in those early years. The city itself was a difficult place to live with high social deprivation and all the associated problems. Waste disposal services were always a constant problem. The school system was difficult and the sheer busyness, noise and corruption of the city took a lot to get used to.

Fuorigrotta

They persevered, however, and along with their team, Eleanor Machray and Mela Finnocchio (sent out from GLO in Australia), began to see results for their work. After two or three years the team came to an end with Mela returning to Australia and Eleanor marrying Adino Ricossa, an Italian farmer from the north of Italy. Eleanor and Adino continued to be active in their area evangelising whilst farming. They hosted many summer teams and evangelised their rural community with the help of book tables at local markets. However, the dispersing of the Naples team meant that Robert and Muriel had to build a new Resident Team using the summer teams as a recruiting ground.

One of Robert's early objectives was to put a gospel of John into every home in Fuorigrotta and the surrounding area, a huge task given that there were 200,000 people living in the area. This project –was launched in 1995 required a constant flow of summer teams to achieve it and that in turn meant teams staying in the Hamilton's own home. It was finally achieved by the turn of the millennium, and with a new church planting project beginning in Pozzuoli, the emphasis shifted to distributing gospels to every home in that area, a population of 50,000. This proved to be a success with many people responding and getting in touch once they had received a gospel and some becoming Christians. One of the converts from this project was a young man called Luca Illiano who, along with his wife Anca, later became a GLO workers.

As the Hamiltons began to rebuild their team, the first new team member was actually a Neopolitan, Patrizio Zucchetto. Patrizio was converted in 1993 during his military service in Florence and returned to get baptised in November of 1994 in the Fuorigrotta church. For two years Robert discipled him and while attending the International Brethren Conference on Mission in Rome in 1996 he developed a burden for Christian ministry. Patrizio then went to train at Tilsley College with a desire to go back and work alongside Robert and Muriel. He married Jennifer, an Irish girl he had met on summer teams and the couple spent ten years working in the church planting project in Pozzuoli. Those years were challenging but the church that resulted now numbers 90 people.

Patrizio eventually returned to the church in Fuorigrotta to help in leadership when the Hamiltons left Italy and continued there, combining church leadership with a training ministry as well as itinerant preaching all over Italy. As a couple he and Jennifer were also involved in reaching the villages and towns in the greater Naples area where there is no gospel witness or church - preparing the ground for new church plants. They have subsequently relocated to the town of Serino.

The next couple to come to Italy were Leo and Angie Isac who had been to Tilsley College in 1993. Leo was Romanian and Angie from Motherwell. They met on the GLO course and married shortly afterwards. With a developing interest in mission they went on several Italian GLO teams before finally committing to go to Naples full-time as missionaries in 2000, initially working with the church in Fuorigrotta in youth work. By this stage Robert and Muriel had planned to have five couples joining them in the work and functioning as a dispersed team involved in more than one church.

The Isacs worked for two and a half years in Naples before leaving to help a small church in Santa Maria a Vico, some 30km north east of Naples. They stayed for four and a half years and were involved in evangelism and leadership. This was followed by an additional two-and-a-half-year stint helping another church further north in Tuscany.

This team was further supplemented by a Faroese couple Regin and Heidi Guttesen, though Heidi was the daughter of American missionaries to the Philippines. They added an extra dimension to the team due to Regin's musical ability as a singer/songwriter. The Guttesens were involved in the Pozzuoli church plant as well and then left to begin a church planting work in Campobasso, a village 160km from Naples in a region where there is no church for the dozens of villages. In addition to evangelism Regin has also released Christian albums in Italian which are a valuable resource for the Italian Church

Two more couples joined the work - Vicky Bibby came as a single woman and met her Albanian husband in Italy. She worked on the team for three years before she and Erion moved up to Marsciano and then back to Vicky's native Wales. Also Joel and Adina Volle were part of the team before returning to the USA. They have subsequently returned to Italy where they are involved in camp work.

Italian Resident Team 2006

The team worked in a dispersed way, involved in several different churches. By the time Robert and Muriel left Naples to return to a pastoral position in a church in Aberdeen and then Newtownards, GLO was firmly established in Italy and had built up a great deal of credibility. The church in Fuorigrotta had also begun to reach out elsewhere by commending others including Berny Tuccillo who worked for a while in Ireland as a missionary, Alessandro Esposito who served in both Zambia and India before returning to Italy and Luca Illiano who along with Anca works in the Mergellina area of the city doing evangelism.

Spain

Spain was another area where activity was taking place. For a number of years a team of New Zealanders worked with a small and fledgling church in Vilagarcía in northern Spain. Following their years at the Training Centre/Tilsley College, Ray and Eunice Cawston decided to return to the mission field but this time to southern Spain and the city of Murcia to work with a small church. They were joined two years later by Luis and Anne-Laure Mostacero.

Ray & Eunice Cawston, Anne-Laure & Luis Mostacero

The team in Murcia saw considerable blessing and growth, not least because of an influx of Latin Americans to the area. After six years, the Mostaceros left to begin a new GLO work in Peru where they were joined by Richard and Pam Harknett. On their departure, the Cawstons were joined by Aurelio and Nani Esquembri who were with them for two years before their retirement. The Esquembris continued to serve in Murcia for another thirteen years.

Summer teams have been held in Spain for many years in Galicia, Guadalajara, Soria, Avila, Malaga, Murcia, Barcelona, and Jumilla. A number of the teams in Soria were led by John Speirs. Summer teams also went to Madrid to work with Ken and Alison Barrett, who are missionaries with Echoes International.

Ireland

Ireland was also an area of expansion for GLO. A team consisting of Guy and Jocelyn Pembroke and Trevor and Julia Chipperfield went to assist the church in South Hill, Dublin which was Trevor's home church and a frequent destination for GLO summer teams. Trevor and the Pembrokes completed the GLO course in 1988/89 before commencing the work in South Hill. The Pembrokes wanted to move on to a new ministry in Peru and following their departure, Linda Bellchamber joined the South Hill team in 1995 after her year in training at Motherwell. The following year she married John Stanfield and they moved to Bethany Church in Dublin where they worked for a year with Colin and Rosemary Sheldon. During that year they became aware of the real need which existed in some of the smaller towns in Ireland where there was little or no evangelical witness. Reggie Fry, an Irish businessman who knew the church scene well encouraged them to move to County Wexford as there were no other missionaries working there. They did so, moving to the town of Enniscorthy which lies on the main road south east from Dublin. Enniscorthy is a riverside town of 8,000 with a surrounding population of 26,000. The only evangelical witness in the town was the joint Presbyterian and Methodist Church, where the minister was a believer, and a few Christians associated with the Quaker Meeting House.

The main focus of their initial evangelism was door-to-door visitation offering evangelistic videos for loan. People in the town were friendly but wary and this proved to be a very effective way of breaking down barriers. At the end of 1997 they also did a mass distribution of gospel calendars in the town and an offer of Christian videos. The following year they distributed a leaflet entitled "Why bother with the Bible?" and this project was completed by the summer mission team which came in August 1998. They also added to their activities by going to the National Ploughing Championship with leaflets for distribution.

The end result of this extensive literature work was a series of Bible studies that were initiated with a young Christian couple and two women who were not believers, as well as some Bible Discovery Groups. Andrew and Lorna Burt (from Scotland) joined the team in January 1999 and they all began a millennium survey and leaflet distribution door-to-door which bore some fruit including a number of people coming to a millennium Bible exhibition. Linda and Lorna ran a women's Bible study group and Lorna also began a ladies' coffee break event as well as some adult literacy work.

Andrew & Lorna Burt

Children's holiday clubs also commenced, and Stephen Blunt (from England) joined the team in 2001 to help in this and other areas of the work. Trudy Yeomans (from Australia) joined in 2003 and she and Stephen eventually married. Andrew's sister Magdalene also joined the team and in addition to her evangelistic responsibilities, she leads the worship at church. It was only to be a matter of time before a church structure would begin to emerge with a Family Service (initially once a month) and also Praise Nights with music and testimonies, and a short gospel message. While this work was being established the team attended a small church fourteen miles away in Wexford town which offered them fellowship. In time, however, with the church in Enniscorthy maturing, that became their focus. The work of church planting proved to be slower than the team had anticipated, Ireland was as challenging a country as anywhere to work, however the church did continue to grow and stabilise.

Children's club in Ireland

In 2008 John and Linda moved to Limerick to join David & Kay Stevens who were working with Mallow Street Christian Fellowship and Berny Tuccillo (who also was with GLO for a period) went and joined them. The Burts remained in Enniscorthy and continued evangelising in the town. Shortly after that Berny married Michaela and this made the team complete. Together they ran many special evangelistic events, women's Bible studies, Alpha courses and did lots of literature distribution. These activities were coupled with street evangelism, schools' work and friendship evangelism.

In August 2013 Berny & Michaela went to Shannon where they developed a children's ministry while the Stanfields continued to help Mallow Church in Limerick. The Burts remained with the church plant in Enniscorthy which has continued to grow and develop.

Scandinavia

Jens and Elin Wang began a new team in the Danish capital Copenhagen, working extensively with the Faroese church in the city. Later, three other couples, the Berghammers, the Hansens and the Fuglos would begin a church plant in Skovlunde which was an extension of the Beroa church in Copenhagen, while Valdemar and Ruth Lützen worked with the Fellowship Church in Copenhagen. This period of mission activity saw a number of summer teams going to Denmark, working with local churches and holding open-air outreaches using drama and music. Subsequently summer teams were sent to Norway and Iceland which have proved useful in building bridges with churches as well as evangelism. While Scandinavia remains a spiritually needy place we currently have no full-time missionaries serving there.

Back at the Centre

With staff leaving the Motherwell Centre to work elsewhere there was need for more to join the team. Joan Schroder retired as secretary and she was replaced by Jan Goodall who lived locally. Jan worked as PA to John Speirs and made an enormous contribution to the work of GLO in this capacity. She was assisted in the admin department over the years by people such as Mark Shufflebottom, Gillian Frew (neé Smith) and Anna McRobert (neé Pinney)

When John retired as European Coordinator Jan continued to assist him in his ministry, while at the same time taking charge of the Conferencing work and a whole range of other supportive tasks. In addition, Jan and Debbie McQuoid run ladies' Precept Bible studies and events at the GLO Centre. These Bible studies provide teaching, fellowship and encouragement for around 50 women from a variety of local churches.

It was important to keep the wider work of GLO together so an International Conference began which involved the leaders of all the major GLO countries. GLO Europe played host in August of 1998 as GLO leaders from Australia, Korea, India, Malaysia, New Zealand and Zambia joined their European counterparts for a time of fellowship and mutual encouragement. The agreement was reached that GLO leaders from around the world would continue to meet up every three or four years to maintain a sense of fellowship and unity. That has continued until the present with the most recent gathering being held in Kuala Lumpur, Malaysia in June of 2023 where 60 GLO International delegates from around a dozen countries around the world came together.

International Conference in Malaysia

As the new millennium approached there were a number of interesting changes. Spearhead took on a new format by growing bigger to A4 format and generally becoming more colourful. There was a genuine desire to make it look more attractive and appealing to a wider readership. In time a student with artistic flair and computer skills would bring an energy and creativity to the admin department. Mark Shufflebottom would work with GLO for several years before he took up university postings in Bournemouth and then Canada. He became the designer for Spearhead which changed its name to e-vision and continues to do so from his base in Toronto.

Vision 2000

One of the developments to take place was a project called 'Vision 2000'. This project was launched in 1995 with the aim of having 100 workers on the field by the year 2000. To facilitate this vision a small Development Group was formed chaired by David Clarkson and included Sam Gibson, Shona Cobham, Catherine Moreau (née King), Colin MacPhie, Geoff Ruston, Graham Hobbs, John Speirs and myself. A consultant by the name of David Cormack was invited to the European Workers' Conference to discuss and explain the issue of development and strategy. This kind of purposeful thinking was unusual in GLO even though personal drive, determination and planning were very much part of GLO culture. There was some discussion on the value of stating a specific target for the year 2000. However, it was felt that the overall impact of such a project would be beneficial and the vast majority of GLO workers were in favour of the project. In reality, the actual figure was not achieved, but there were many benefits, not least because it forced everyone in GLO to reflect on the importance of growth, moving forward and planning in mission.

At the end of 1996 Sam and Andrea Gibson and their family returned to Northern Ireland and as a direct outcome of the Development Group, Sam was appointed to the role of Mission Coordinator for GLO. This became the next step in the ongoing evolution of GLO's structure.

Another interesting spin-off of these discussions was some reflection on GLO's relationship with the Brethren movement. While everyone was aware of GLO's church heritage, there was also a recognition that many churches with a Brethren background no longer identified themselves in that way. GLO was also attracting the attention and support of churches and individuals from other church backgrounds. The Development Group gave some thought to this and it was agreed that GLO would be willing to accept workers from any church provided they complied with some basic core principles. Those principles were listed as:

- Autonomy of the local church
- Plurality of leadership
- The Lord's Supper celebrated regularly
- Believer's baptism by immersion

These core values were subsequently incorporated into the GLO Workers' Handbook.

Another aspect worth nothing in the years preceding the new millennium was the growing relationship with both Echoes and Interlink. Relationships had taken time to develop but by this stage there was both good communication and co-operation between the three organisations. It was felt that there should also be a public demonstration of unity and a plan was launched to hold three joint events in the year 2000 which would be called mission awareness days. One would take place in England on 1 April 2000, one in Scotland on the

8 April and one in Northern Ireland on the 15 April. Each of these days was well attended and the benefits of co-operating together were becoming more and more obvious.

UK ventures

In the UK some co-operative ventures were launched. Thornhill Church in Cardiff were looking for someone to be involved in evangelism and one couple who were interested in this were Alex and Jennifer Wilson. An agreement was reached whereby they worked with Thornhill as GLO workers. Andy and Claire Gibson were also interested in joining GLO and being involved in a church plant. They went to Hereford to work with Martin and Rachel Erwin who were Counties workers. In addition, in 1998 GLO joined forces with Counties and UKET (later to become the CGT) to form the Church Planting Initiative (CPI) - an organisation that would support church planting in the UK. During its lifetime CPI was to have some success in encouraging church planting as well as consolidating relationships between the missionary service groups, including Partnership who would join up later.

The year 2001 saw Ian and Jenny Smith join GLO to work in the admin department. Ian would eventually become Treasurer, but his heart for Albania would help to keep that needy country in mind. Jenny would put her computer skills to good use as well as play a major role in the administration of the summer teams before pursuing a career in teaching.

The work of refurbishment of the Motherwell Centre continued, this time a partition wall was erected at the back of the sports hall so that the College library could have more space and an additional 72 metre of shelving were added. Also much needed space for the bookshop was increased by 30% following different configuration. All of this was achieved with the help of a Brass Tacks team. One of the interesting spin offs from this was that one of the Brass Tacks volunteers, Dani Bianchi, later came to Tilsley College as a student.

Greater Glasgow

New projects continued to develop in central Scotland as well. Over in Johnstone, a post-industrial town to the east of Glasgow, a small church situated just off the main street had just closed its doors in 1998. Bobby and

Mairi Sneddon who lived in the area were determined that a Christian witness should be maintained there. Bobby came to Tilsley College in 1999 while his wife Mairi worked in a council run care facility. Following Bobby's training they joined GLO and began to replant the church there. They were joined full-time by John and Fiona Dick and benefitted from the input of Tilsley College students. Bobby & Mairi's daughter, Joanne, worked in Johnstone for several years. Dimity Street Church has grown and continues to reach out to the local community including local schools.

Johnstone holiday club

Meanwhile the elders of a church in Renfrew, not far from Johnstone, approached GLO to see if they could get any help as they tried to develop their church in what was a growing urban population area. Just at that time a couple, Brian and Liz Hawthorne, were studying at Tilsley College. Liz had a long involvement with GLO as she used to regularly go on Donegal summer teams with Nelson Logan. The couple were asked if they would be interested in joining GLO and also work with the church in Renfrew. They felt this was

God's guidance and so for some years a three-way relationship existed that saw Brian and Liz working as evangelists in the church and also involved in schools' work in the local community as well as hosting summer teams.

Committee representation

With the passing of time comes changing expectations. It was becoming very obvious to people within the work as well as onlookers, that the GLO Committee was all male. Quite apart from appearances this was clearly unreflective of GLO's workforce, more than half of whom were women. The Committee, having delayed a decision for some time, decided to appoint two women at the same time. The rationale was that if just one woman was appointed then it would put unreasonable pressure on her. Consequently, Senga Lake who was on the 1975 GLO team to Rome and had lots of mission experience along with Karen Macrae, who had done many teams in both Spain and France, were duly appointed to the Main Committee. Another first occurred the following year when Sarah Gibson, having graduated from Tilsley College, was employed for a two-year period to represent the work of GLO nationally.

It was becoming clear that GLO's different ministries were beginning to have an impact far beyond the immediate ministries of GLO. Missionaries like Valerie Kyle, Chrissie Mulindabigwi and Stephanie Lannon had previously either been on GLO summer teams or they had studied at Tilsley College and were now doing an invaluable work on the mission field. Young people were returning from summer teams fired up with a renewed desire for evangelism in their local area. Moreover, churches across the UK and Europe had leaders and other key people who had studied at Tilsley College before returning to secular employment and were utilising their learning to be a blessing in their local church.

Chapter 8

More Recent Times

Sabbaticals are a rarity in GLO but when they have happened they have proved to be a blessing, often for surprising reasons. In 2007 I was contacted by a friend, Allan McKinnon who was serving as a missionary in Tanzania along with his wife Jacqui. They had been hosts to a number of GLO summer teams so knew GLO fairly well. Allan wanted to finish off a Master's degree in education at Glasgow University and so wanted to find cover for a Bible college he had established in the town of Moshi where they lived. We spent six months as a family in Tanzania while Allan and Jacqui came to Scotland in an exchange with Allan joining the Tilsley College staff. It did not take long to realise the fit was good and two years later when Allan and Jacqui finally left Tanzania, Allan accepted an invitation to become a permanent feature of the Tilsley College staff, becoming Academic Dean and then College Principal.

Sheila Park, who along with her husband Alan had been a missionary in Zambia, also joined the college as librarian and for a couple years was College Administrator. Another newcomer Erika Raigné came from Patagonia, Argentina. She had sensed God's calling since childhood to be a missionary and applied to study at Tilsley College. She arrived following four months of work in Barcelona to raise the funds for the course. After the course she investigated a variety of openings in the mission field but stayed at Tilsley College to work in administration and lecturing and combining this with schools' work in Central Scotland with MAD Ministries (Making a Difference), before going on to work with IBCM.

Added to this growing group of college staff were Simon and Dorit Marshall who met on the GLO course in 1980/81 before going on to a variety of mission roles. They attended the International Brethren Conference on Mission in Strasbourg in 2011 where several GLO Board members were also in attendance. In conversations that took place at that Conference it became clear that Simon and Dorit should return to Motherwell and join the staff. Simon served as a lecturer at the college, then its principal while Dorit worked in administration. Simon then handed over the principalship to Allan McKinnon and went on to work with ECMI. Georgette Short took over as academic dean.

Three more people joined the team around that time at Tilsley College and served for a number of years on a part time basis. Jim Crooks who had been a visiting lecturer for many years as well as a member of the College Council joined the staff with a particular role to develop the Joshua Project and take responsibility for the development of e-learning. He brought with him experience from many years in further education. David Wilson, a local church elder was taken on to help with college administration and student placements and combined this with practical help around the Centre. David continues to volunteer in the bookshop.

The third person to join was Garry Blair who combined an itinerant preaching ministry and leadership in a local church with work in the college as a lecturer.

College staff

Latest recruits

The college has always been refreshed over the years with new people and that has continued to be the case. Seb and Jess Brandt, a young French couple came and joined the team for a time before pursuing their career with GEM. Gareth Armstrong and Ruth Young also joined the college, Gareth as a lecturer and Ruth as Practical Placements Tutor. They each combined their college roles with an involvement in summer teams and church ministries. Those joining the college team in recent years include David Irvine who, as well as lecturing, is the Pastoral Lead, José Junior as Academic Dean and Paul Wilson.

It was not just the college that benefitted from new people, the GLO Centre as a whole benefited. Judith McKeown got to know about GLO by doing summer teams and so she applied to Tilsley College to become a student. After the course she took on a dual role helping in the college and also administering the short-term mission teams. She now combines her work on short-term teams with an international student ministry. There was also a need for a Centre Manager who would take responsibility for the physical infrastructure of the GLO Centre. After an appeal to local churches, Charlie and Tania Deering, missionaries to Ecuador and then Spain, joined GLO where Charlie took on the role of Centre Manager and Tania caters for the students.

New era

The issue of succession planning had been discussed at several Board meetings. It was agreed that executive Board members should retire at the age of 65. While this policy had never been implemented it served as a guide. John Speirs retired as European Coordinator aged 67 in 2011 and transitioned into an ambassadorial role which lasted for a few years. I was asked by the GLO Main Committee to take up the role but with the title of General Director of GLO.

This was part of a restructuring in which the Committee would formally become a Board with executive directors and non-executive members. As part of this new structure three departments would be recognised each with its own director. Sam Gibson would be Mission Director, Mark Davies Training Director and Ian Smith the Finance Director. As time went on Allan McKinnon joined the Executive Team as the Principal of Tilsley College and most recently Richard Harknett joined as Regional Training Director. Together we form an Executive Team with Allison Hill as Secretary to the Board. While the complete GLO Board, to whom we are all accountable, continued to meet three times a year, we as Directors met at least six times a year to keep the engine of GLO ticking over.

John Speirs handing over to Stephen McQuoid

One of the first tasks that the new team of Directors had to attend to was the development of a coherent strategy for GLO. John Hunter, who was still Chairman of GLO at the time of this transition, attended the early Directors' meetings and put a considerable amount of time and thought into articulating possible ways forward for the organisation. With the process of succession complete, John Hunter also brought to an end his tenure as Board Chairman having served on the Board for 27 years.

The Directors then produced a strategic plan which the Board approved after some discussion. In one sense the strategic plan was not new in that it did represent what had been done over the past number of years. However, it expressed GLO's purpose in a way that was clear and concise. In summary it stated that the overall function of GLO was to 'grow mission-focused churches in Europe' and that this would be achieved through 'evangelism, establishing churches and church ministries, training people for service and resourcing all of the activity mentioned above. Four words: **Evangelise, Establish, Train and Resource**, were to become the bywords that described GLO and its activity.

Getting the message

With the new leadership in place and the challenge of recruiting young people for mission, there was a need for a specific focus on summer teams and that meant recruiting someone whose sole purpose was to recruit for these teams. Adi Harris, an elder at Greenview Evangelical Church in Glasgow, had taken a break from work in his battle with cancer. During his seven-year phase of treatment and surgery he gained a theology degree at International Christian College and was open to some form of Christian service. He joined GLO on a part time basis to head up the short-term mission teams programme. Sadly Adi passed away, but his contribution during the time he was with us was invaluable. In order to assist communication, a media ministry was begun and local film maker Gordon McLeod, also joined the work of GLO. Brian and Iris Gooding also joined GLO on a part-time basis to assist in pastoral care.

Spearhead magazine continued to be the main publicity engine for GLO with a circulation of some 3500. However, it was felt that the term 'Spearhead' was becoming a little anachronistic. The content had developed over the years and in its present format it was a 16-page magazine that not only informed the reader of the work of GLO but also sought to educate people on issues such as current trends, missiological developments and the current spiritual situation in Europe. The title had to be changed to reflect a changing world. A competition was held at the GLO Workers' Conference of 2013 and lots of different names were suggested. After a significant amount of deliberation the name 'e-vision' was arrived at. It was felt that this name suggested both a European focus and well as a desire for a visionary approach to mission.

Land of the eagle

One of the most exciting locations to have developed in recent years is that of Albania. Just a handful of years ago Albania was one of the most repressive Communist regimes on earth. Robert Hamilton, while working in Italy remembers standing on the east coast of Italy and looking over the Adriatic to Albania and wondering if that country would ever open up to the gospel.

Prayers were answered and in the early 1990s the country became a democracy and allowed for freedom of religion.

Italian Christians were among the first to respond to this new openness by sending missionaries to evangelise and plant churches. In the northern city of Shköder a church was planted and Thomas and Anna D'Andrea had an involvement in the work there along with Peter Hedley, an Echoes missionary to Italy. Graham Hobbs who had been a GLO Board member also maintained an active interest in the Shköder work.

Ian Smith also had an interest in Albania, though his initial involvement was to take much needed relief to Albanian Christians who were living in significant poverty as well as being a trustee of an orphanage in the town of Gjirokastër. He also got in touch with a newly established church in the southern city of Vlorë and this is where the GLO work in Albania would consolidate.

Civil war broke out in Albania which made travel to the country difficult and dangerous. However once this was over Ian re-established relationships with the church in Vlorë and in 2006 a young woman, Jona Duka, was sent to Tilsley College to train. Jona returned to Vlorë and got a job with World Vision and the relationship between the church and GLO began to develop, helped also by summer teams and GLO workers coming to help with church camps.

In 2008 the church sent a young couple, Juli and Ela Muhameti, to Tilsley College with the expressed wish that they would come back and work in the city once more. They did so, returning as GLO workers, involved in leadership in the church, university evangelism and also helping to start a church plant just down the road in the neighbouring town of Orikum. Another Albanian couple, Ermal and Denisa Bimaj took the same route a couple of years later and now the two couples work together as a team in Vlorë.

The work in Vlorë has grown from strength to strength. One of the big challenges they face is that many Albanian young people try to leave the country to find work elsewhere. That has meant a continual steam of young converts being discipled, helping out in the church for a short while and then moving permanently abroad. Despite this, the church has continually grown. It has also demonstrated both flexibility and tenacity. For example, during the Covid pandemic, their little church building was closed by the authorities due to its unsuitability, undeterred the church began meeting for a time in a forest next to the city.

Muhameti family

Bimaj family

Meeting in the forest

A recent development which was a real encouragement was that the church found a much better building near to the city centre. They began to raise funds for the purchase and were helped by GLO to contact donors in the UK. Finally in the spring of 2023 they took possession of the building and hosted some GLO teams to help with practical building and refurbishment work. The new premises are ideal not only because they provide adequate space for Sunday services and youth work, but also because summer teams can also be accommodated in the building.

Developments in Italy

The Italian work also continued to develop. A young man from the church at Naples called Luca Illiano had gone to live in London. Luca's ambition had been to be an artist but while in the UK he developed a burden to go back to Naples and begin a church planting work in the area of Mergellina where he had grown up. Supported by his new church in St Albans he came to Tilsley College and was then commended to return to Naples. Luca is now married to Anca who is from Romania and together they do evangelism in the Mergellina area as well as using Luca's interest in art and sculpture as a way of communicating the gospel.

Luca doing art evangelism

Zucchetto family

Having spent years working in Naples, Patrizio and Jennifer felt burdened to leave the city and begin church planting in the province of Avellino one hour east of Naples. They settled in the town of Serino which had no evangelical church and began pioneering evangelism using book tables, literature distribution, English classes and working with the local migrant community. The Covid pandemic made life challenging, but they persevered and a small church was established meeting in their home. It was not long before the church outgrew the space and now they have acquired a permanent building in which to meet.

Moving East

Another important development began in Eastern and Central Europe. Roger Brind of the Philadelphia Trust had been travelling to Eastern Europe as far back as the days of the Iron Curtain to encourage Christians, run camps and do Bible teaching. He approached GLO for help so that some of the many needs he identified could be addressed. Initially it was through the use of summer teams which added to the evangelistic efforts that were already in process. Soon training became an even bigger issue. In the Hungarian village of Dömös there was a small Bible centre that was supported by the Wiedenest Mission from Germany and also by the Philadelphia Trust. GLO was invited to join in a multilateral training work. The idea was to establish a small weekend-based training school to help Hungarian speaking Christians both from Hungary itself and also the Hungarian speaking parts of Romania, Slovakia and the Ukraine. The first Board meeting for the Dömös Bible School was held in Wiedenest, Germany in 2011. The members included Christof Stenker and Mattais Schmidt from Wiedenest, Ernoe Nagy and Janos Harmatta from the Dömös Bible Centre, Roger Brind and Paul Thomas from the Philadelphia Trust and myself from GLO. Later on Mark Davies and Richard Harknett picked up the connection on behalf of GLO

From these early beginnings the work in Eastern and Central Europe developed. Following the success of the work at of Dömös and also that of Philadelphia Trust's International Conference, churches from other Central and Eastern European countries asked for help. At this point GLO and Philadelphia Trust approached Echoes International and the three bodies agreed to develop a training ministry that would help these churches by organising structured and systematic training trips to these locations. To date, training events have been held in Romania, Albania, Ukraine, Hungary, Chechia, Slovakia, Slovenia and Poland.

Eastern European team

One of the positive outcomes from this have been Church Leaders' Consultations. These are gatherings in which we bring together some of the key church leaders we are working with and supporting so we can provide them with some intensive training as well as having a time of sharing, prayer and fellowship. The first of these was held in the Bible Centre in Domos at which about 60 attended. To date there have been three consultations, the most recent with 100 in attendance from 12 different countries.

Another development of this was GLO people being used by a range of organisations to help them with training. This was encouraged as we always wanted to demonstrate a generous spirit towards others. Both IBCM and the European Leadership Forum make good use of GLO people and this has proved to be a mutually beneficial arrangement.

Hungary

One country that we were able to consolidate following our eastward move was Hungary. Robert and Emese Lemperger were a couple from the university city of Eger who ran a Christian publishing ministry. Robert was also the leader of a small church in the city. Following some initial contact they began hosting short-term mission teams to Hungary. These ran for some years before they expressed an interest in joining the work of GLO. Their ministry continues to be around the publishing of gospel literature as well as a Christian magazine for Hungary and the Hungarian speaking diaspora, as well as translating and publishing key biblical and theological books. They also continue to lead short-term mission teams as well as promote the work of GLO throughout Hungary.

Lemperger family

Darnley Mill

While these news fields were opening up overseas, progress continued to be made back in Scotland. I wrote to dozens of churches in the central belt expressing a desire to see more churches planted and asked them to contact me if they were interested in a conversation about it. There were a number of responses, including one from Greenview Evangelical Church where Allan

McKinnon was an elder. The end result was that a church plant was born in the Darnley area of South Glasgow.

A team was brought together which included , James and Linda McKerlie, Allan and Jacqui McKinnon and Ruth Young. They initially met in a pub-restaurant which was then closed due to the Covid pandemic. When things began to open up again they relocated to a unit on an industrial estate.

Working in partnership

With training developing in Europe, it was time to develop it further in the UK also. One of the consequences of working closely with sister organisations such as Echoes International, Counties and Partnership was that within GLO we became aware of the training these other organisations were involved in. After a great deal of discussion it was agreed that there should be some working together so as to provide support for churches in the UK. A small think tank called the National Training Network (later named Enable training) was formed. In addition a wider group of mission service agencies began meeting (initially called the Service Group Forum now called the Church Support Network). Each organisation committed to working together and support one another wherever appropriate. As relationships continued to develop it was agreed that in order to facilitate good communication and co-operation, the Chair and CEO's of some of the organisations would get together every six months to touch base. Currently these groups include Counties, Echoes International, Church Growth Trust and GLO.

All of these developments coincided with a longstanding desire among the GLO Board to have a base in the south of England. It was decided that Mark would continue as Training Director, overseeing all the training work of GLO, but he and Shirley would relocate to London from where they could advance the work of GLO and also develop these national training initiatives. Mark began to pursue an itinerant teaching ministry taking him throughout the country. He and Shirley also got involved in the ministry of Highgate International Church where Mark became an elder.

Over the next few years Mark would spearhead GLO training in England and Wales and would be assisted in this by Richard Harknett who along with his wife Pam who had returned from Peru where they were GLO missionaries.

A number of Joshua courses were run as well as day seminars and both Mark and Richard were involved in training initiatives with our partner organisation Counties as well as helping with workshops at the Living the Passion conferences that GLO was involved with. Highgate Church also saw growth, albeit from a very low base, and then Mark and Shirley relocated to Northampton where they continue their GLO ministry.

Aix-en-Provence team

Old fields and new opportunities

New projects were also developing in some of the more established locations. Philippe and Marie-Christine Perrilliat had a burden to move on from Marseille and begin a new church plant, this time in the university town of Aix-en-Provence some 30km north of Marseille. This was part of an ambitious nationwide initiative to establish a church for every 10,000 members of the French population. They initially teamed up with another experienced missionary couple, Brad and Catherine Dickson who had worked in Grenoble for many years. The project is intended to be multi-faceted. At its heart would be the church plant, but the two couples also intend to attract a larger team of young people who can learn about church planting by participating in

Aureille family Eva & Mayeul

the team and then to branch out to plant other churches in the region and beyond. This in turn would be coupled with a ministry to the 35,000 students who are linked the University of Aix. This combination of church plant, training ministry and student work could prove to be a template for the future.

The work in Aix-en-Provence grew and now there is a thriving church there. One of the exciting developments from this work was that a young couple who came to Aix to learn about church planting, Ben and Anne-Aymone Suter, went to the nearby town of Salon-de-Provence and have planted a church there also. Meanwhile Philippe's ministry continues to grow with youth camps being run each year in Belgium and also helping to mentor and guide leaders of established churches in the region.

Another exciting development began to take shape in Marseille, a city in the South of France where GLO has had a long link. One of the churches planted in Marseille was Le Cep which had grown to about 180. The church was looking to expand and so got in touch with GLO so we could partner together. Several things began to develop. First, one of the elders of Le Cep, Mayeul Aureille and his wife Eva came to the UK for a sabbatical and spent time both at the GLO Centre in Motherwell and in Devon. They joined GLO as missionaries and then returned to Marseille to lead new initiatives. Then the church opened a café in the very centre of the city called 'Bulle2cafe' from which they can run outreaches and café church events. They are also developing a missional community in Aubagne with plans to grow it into a church.

The Balkans is one of the great mission needs in Europe as well as a challenging place to be in ministry. There was a growing burden within the GLO leadership that we should begin to venture into this area and pray that God would open doors for us. As a direct result of these prayers and visits to the region we got in touch with a Slovene couple, Boštjan and Lidija Cifer who live in the city of Maribor where Boštjan is a pastor. We pray that this is the start of greater things in Slovenia and the Balkans.

Moving forward

The work of GLO continues, but in a climate that is very different to the one that existed 50 years ago. Evangelicalism has been in decline in the UK over the past 50 years, though not as quickly as the decline experienced in the established Anglican, Roman Catholic and Presbyterian churches. The decline has not been even across the entire denominational spectrum and Pentecostalism in particular has experienced significant growth. While there is now evidence that the decline may be slowing down it remains the case that churches in the UK are still closing and many of those that remain open are in survival mode. It would also be fair to say that with so many churches now focussed on their own spiritual health, there has also been a general decline in mission interest.

There is also a big change in the way mission is perceived by the church at large. There is a worrying trend to downplay the role of evangelism and even see it as an imposition, especially if it is an overt form of evangelism. This is coupled with a greater interest in social concern and social justice issues as well as an interest in the majority world. The result is that if we were to organise a team to help with an agricultural project in Ethiopia, or to run a soup kitchen in Kolkata or a sanctuary in the Philippines for victims of people trafficking, the team would be filled easily and there would be more than enough donations raised to pay for it all. On the other hand, if we tried to get a team to do street evangelism in Hungary, Spain or worse still a UK location, the team would need to be marketed very well and it would still be a struggle to fill, even though these locations may arguably have greater spiritual needs.

In other European countries the situation has been very different. France, Spain and Italy along with several other European countries have witnessed a growth in the evangelical church, albeit from a very low base. Much of this has been due to consistent missionary activity in these countries over the years. The church has also come of age and now there are encouraging numbers of nationals from these countries entering Christian ministry and mission work. The net result of these changes for GLO is that today we are just as likely to see French, Italian, Albanian or Spanish national workers joining GLO as missionaries as we are to see people from the UK taking this step.

The challenges are great and indeed the Europe of today is arguably a more complex and more challenging a place to witness than the Europe of 50 years ago. Secularism is now endemic within the cultures of most European countries and the hedonism that often accompanies a secularised culture is also widespread. The historic faiths of Roman Catholicism and the Orthodox churches are increasingly irrelevant. People may be culturally Catholic or Orthodox but that does not translate into an active faith. Young people in particular have abandoned these churches and treat them with a degree of contempt. Meanwhile Islam is growing rapidly in Europe, encouraged by immigration and biological growth as much as by conversion. It is to this Europe that GLO is called to minister.

GLO's vision is to 'grow mission focused churches in Europe'. Our intention is to do this this through evangelism, establishing of churches, training and resourcing mission. Given that 800 million Europeans don't know Christ and the increasing resistance to the gospel, the work of GLO is needed more now than ever.

Chapter 9

Lessons from the Memory Banks

As I reflect back over the past 50 years of GLO history, not only are there many things to thank God for, but there are also many lessons that I think we can learn from all that has happened. These will, I believe, help to prepare us for the next 50 years if God spares us. I describe these lessons in random order.

Hard... but not Impossible

The first and perhaps most obvious lesson from the past 50 years is that Europe is a very hard mission field. I feel this needs to be stated because it amplifies the heroism of GLO missionaries who have given their lives to reaching Europeans for Christ. During the course of my ministry I have had the privilege of preaching, evangelising and lecturing in many countries around the world. This has given me an insight into how spiritually different much of the world is from Europe. I remember preaching at a mission in Congo when, after one altar call, 11 people came forward to accept Christ. I have done door-to-door work with students from the GLO Centre in Zambia and have witnessed people readily accept Christ there too. In Europe, however, those kind of results just don't happen! The resistance that is encountered when doing evangelism in Europe is immense. There are many layers of suspicion, latent religious dogma, scepticism, and apathy to penetrate before we can really impact people with the gospel. All of this together makes evangelism and church planting in Europe a very tough prospect. It takes time, great patience and perseverance and of course energy because it is simply very hard work.

That said it is not impossible. I say this because as we look back over five decades of mission work, we can see churches throughout Europe that did not exist 50 years ago. There are also many believers serving God today in various parts of Europe who did not grow up in Christian families and had no church association but were contacted and befriended by GLO missionaries or team members and through that relationship came to know Christ for themselves. The evidence is there all over Europe that people can be reached and challenged with the claims of Christ and can come into a living faith with him.

Don't fear failure

A second lesson is that we should not be afraid of failure. Anyone who has studied the history of mission will know that there has always been an element of failure in the task of mission. In a fallen world we should expect opposition. Yet there are victories too. Indeed every person who becomes a Christian is an enormous victory because they have been snatched from the Kingdom of Darkness. By God's grace we overcome, but often our greatest victories are won in the context of defeats. This is certainly true of Europe. There are countless situations where a missionary has invested years in witnessing to a neighbour or other contact and yet the person never becomes a Christian, church plants that were meticulously planned and worked at diligently, yet never came into fruition, summer teams that were creative and energetic, yet there was no result for all the work. Failure and disappointment in a tough place such as Europe are all part of the package.

Bearing this in mind, there are two approaches that mission groups can take. They can either play it safe or take risks. Playing it safe might sound like the sensible option, but if that is your tendency then church planting in Europe is something you should never even contemplate. Alternatively, we can be willing to take risks, trust God and be willing to venture into the unknown. We might end up with some failure, but if we are not willing to take risks we will never reach people with the gospel. There needs to be a willingness to try that summer team even if most of the tracts will end up in the bin, have that open air even if people seem to walk by, begin that church plant even if we fear it might not succeed. Only when we have that adventurous spirit will we be able to place ourselves in the vulnerable position of relying entirely on God to bless.

Flexibility

Linked with this is the need for flexibility. In GLO's history there have been church plants that did not last - yet those who were converted went on to serve God in other places. At other times a church was planted and then amalgamated into another one - in the process people became Christians so God's work continued even if not in the way that was initially envisaged. Fixed ideas and inflexible plans are of little value in a world that is rapidly changing and a mission situation that is fluid. We need to have the flexibility to respond to whatever situation confronts us rather than just falling back on old habits and patterns.

Inspire

Fourthly there is an important lesson about inspiration. Mission will always be tough, there needs to be a willingness on the part of people involved in mission to make that sacrifice in order to serve God. Because of this people need to be inspired. One of the remarkable strengths of Colin Tilsley was that he was able to inspire people all over the world. He populated the mission field by challenging people to get involved and gave them a vision of what could be. Within GLO we need to maintain that heritage. Being boring is easy! Many churches and leaders manage to specialise in being humdrum. As a ministry we need to inspire so as to motivate a new generation of missionaries. Ultimately inspiration is not about the quality of an organisation's brochures or the level of interactivity of their website. It is about the people in that organisation. What inspires people is passion, conviction, a sense of purpose and servant leadership. It is here where GLO as an organisation needs to succeed. We do not have a limitless budget when it comes to publicity, but like Colin Tilsley, we can inspire others by our love for Christ, passion for mission and courage to continue in the face of great obstacles.

Training

Lessons must also be learned from training. It is the element of training that takes someone with passion and fine-tunes their skills so as to make them more effective. One of the single most important things a mission organisation can do for its workers is to provide training that truly equips. Of course the nature of training is important. Over the years we have learned that the best way to train someone for mission is not just to fill their heads with knowledge, but rather to combine the theoretical with practical experience and do this in the context of a community where trainees share their lives with each other. This has been the secret of Tilsley College. Students have studied the Bible, theology and ministry skills, but they have also done mission together by visiting mission situations, done evangelising together and helping local churches. In addition the community life component has moulded and built lifelong friendships. It is this combination of influences within a residential course that changes lives and is of greater value that any external academic accreditation, however useful that may be.

Teams

We have also learned a great deal over the years about the importance of teams. It has not always been possible in our history to work in teams. What is more, the teams we have assembled have not always functioned in the same way. Some have been fairly devolved and met irregularly, others were tight knit and met up frequently. But wherever teams have operated, their benefits have been obvious. Working together in a team is not always easy; humility and a willingness to listen to others is an absolute prerequisite, but they have given GLO a real core strength and have been an attractive feature of our work.

Short-term mission

A lesson not to be forgotten is the value of short-term mission teams which have played an enormous role in the history of GLO. Over the years, thousands of people have been exposed to mission by going on one of our summer teams. Many Resident missionaries serving today with GLO and other mission groups will testify that they first got a burden for mission while on a short-term team. They have arguably been the best recruiting tool, both for students for Tilsley College and for long-term GLO workers.

These short-term teams offer numerous benefits and considering they normally only last for two weeks or less, they are very accessible. Among the benefits are the fact that a team can be the arms and legs of the Resident missionaries and can do a huge amount of distribution in a short space of time. They also provide vital manpower for a range of evangelistic activities such as open airs, children's clubs, international evenings and English-speaking classes. The teams are of great benefit to team members themselves and act as a de-facto discipleship programme. Daily Bible studies, prayer times and the engagement in evangelism means that spiritual growth becomes a natural output of short-term team life. So important are the short-term mission teams that it is inconceivable to imagine GLO functioning without them.

Sell the vision and keep selling it relentlessly!

Another important lesson is that people and churches are often taken up with the immediate and when pressures pile up, often the first thing to be forgotten is mission. We should not be surprised by this because life, including church life, brings all sorts of pressures. It does mean that we need to keep pushing the idea of mission and in particularly the importance of reaching people who are unchurched and need to hear the gospel. Organisations like GLO need to have a vision for mission and that vision needs to be constantly communicated. There needs to be a relentlessness about encouraging the church to step up and fulfil the Great Commission. Without this, the gospel imperative will eventually get squeezed out by a whole collection of other issues.

Look to the Next Generation

It is also vital that we keep looking to the next generation. Time never stands still and it affects us all. Mission movements like GLO grow old and need continually refreshed. I am profoundly grateful for people who have joined the work of GLO and have stayed with us for decades. These long-term missionaries have been the backbone of the movement and we should rejoice in the commitment of people who have expended their lives for the cause of mission. However, if we don't find a next generation to continue the work and shoulder the responsibility, GLO like any mission movement will come to an end.

Every generation brings its own strengths and weaknesses. Every new generation will also want to do things differently. This is a good thing provided that the core vision is maintained. What is also evident is that the process of handing on the responsibility does not happen automatically. We need to be intentional about finding the next generation, motivating and empowering them, giving them guidance and supporting them. We also need to learn to entrust them and be willing to let go so that they can carry the vision into the future. This process cannot begin too early, we need to be futureproofing by planning for the future all the time.

Centrality of the Gospel

The final lesson we must learn from our history is the importance of the gospel. GLO has achieved many things by God's grace, but at the heart of what we do is the proclamation of the gospel. In today's world it is less fashionable that 'doing good' or engaging in 'social justice'. Of course doing good is also part of our calling as we follow Jesus, but not at the expense of evangelism. The pendulum has swung too far and many evangelical Christians are hesitant to overtly share the gospel, probably because it is an offense to those that hear it. But the world needs Christ! Europe needs to repent and find forgiveness and that will never happen unless we take seriously our responsibility to go into all the world and make disciples. Evangelism has always been a foundational instinct within GLO and that passion is what has always motivated us. We need to learn from that and go forward into the next 50 years with an unapologetic desire to proclaim the gospel to a continent that is lost.

A Final Word

I hope that as you read this book you will have been inspired by what God has done in and through the work of GLO over the past 50 years. However, the job is far from complete. Europe remains one of the most spiritually needy places on earth. Our desire is to do all we can to reach people for Christ and to raise a new generation of witnesses to do this with us.

In order for us to achieve our goal we need your help. Please partner with us as we seek to reach lost people for Christ. You can do so in the following ways:

1. Pray for us.

2. Inform your church about what GLO is doing.

3. Become a mission Champion (regional rep) for GLO.

4. Join a short-term mission team and encourage others to do so also.

5. Encourage and support students at Tilsley College.

6. Take a personal interest in one of our Resident Teams.

7. Financially support the work of GLO.

8. Join us and become a GLO worker.

For further information contact: admin@glo-europe.org

Also Available

From The GLO Bookshop Motherwell
and all good bookshops

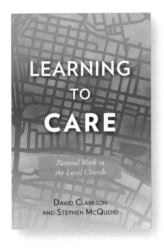

LEARNING TO CARE: Pastoral Work in the Local Church

By David Clarkson and Stephen McQuoid
Paperback 250 pages RRP £9.99
ISBN 9781916013087

People involved in church life expect to be cared for, practically, emotionally and spiritually. Even the secular world sees churches as places of practical and emotional care, a component in the social capital that all societies need. But people are often critical of the pastoral care that churches give in practice, and lack of such care is often the reason given as to why individuals part company with particular churches and the Christian faith in general.

Many churches often struggle to provide the pastoral care that they would like to give. Even when there is a pastor or minister, they can feel overwhelmed by the needs. Some churches rely on leaders who have secular jobs and little opportunity for training in pastoral skills. They are only too well aware of the need to improve the pastoral care that they give.

This book seeks to advise on how the resources of time and spiritual gift across congregations as a whole can be nurtured and deployed to improve pastoral care. It encourages what might be called 360-degree care, from every member to every member.

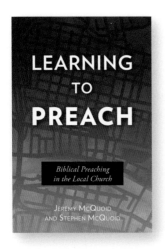

LEARNING TO PREACH: Biblical Preaching in the Local Church

By Jeremy McQuoid and Stephen McQuoid
Paperback 133 pages RRP £8.99
ISBN 9781916013018

It has long been the case that many Christian preachers have learned to preach simply by doing it. Eventually, many have found their way to reasonable competence, but only through much longsuffering on the part of their hearers!

This method, however, carries the risk that preachers will simply reinforce bad habits and practice as well as good ones. The fact is that much can be learned about preaching, both through books and in the classroom, provided the learning is coupled with practice that is constructively criticized both by the preacher and others.

This book has been written with the simple aim of helping self-taught amateur preachers, and novice preachers, to improve. And those who have had some preaching training, whether at Bible school or in other ways, will find it helpful as a refresher. Why not use it as a textbook for training preachers in the local church and in other local groups?

> "Learning to Preach *is a welcome contribution to the growing resources which are available for those who, without much support, are called upon to preach. In a single volume it seeks to span the most important themes which are essential for any preacher, and it is an accessible and motivating book that we hope will be widely used".*
> — Jonathan Lamb, founding Director of Langham Preaching

LEARNING TO SHARE THE GOOD NEWS:
Evangelism and the Local Church

By Stephen McQuoid
Paperback 178 pages RRP £9.99
ISBN 9780957017771

Many would agree that the greatest challenge facing ordinary churches and ordinary Christians in western society today is how to spread the gospel and how to ensure that on a daily basis people are professing Christ for the first time. This book addresses that challenge head-on.

It does so, first, by looking closely at the context in which we evangelise and the varying world-views of those we are trying to reach; and, second, it suggests how individual Christians can involve themselves in the lives and thinking of un-churched people, so as to win them to Christ.

> *"(This book) is full of practical suggestions on how to make the most of opportunities and how to develop strategies for evangelism in and through the local church. It also looks at the difficult questions that emerge in discussion with non-Christians, whether seekers or not, and how they can be answered.*
>
> *The breadth of Stephen's wide reading and research, something that he is so good at, makes the book very valuable not merely because of the subject but the way he organises the results of his research and presents it with clarity and with relevant questions to think about or discuss".* — Roger Chilvers, Evangelist

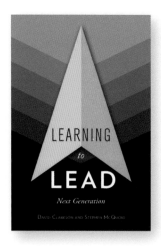

LEARNING TO LEAD: Next Generation

By David Clarkson and Stephen McQuoid
Paperback 182 pages RRP £6.99
ISBN 9781907098154

Our world is facing a leadership crisis at every level – in government, commerce and society at large. The church is not exempt from this and cries out for a new generation of men and women willing to come forward and pick up the leadership baton.

Learning to Lead is written by church leaders for church leaders. It seeks to encourage the pursuit of excellence and prepare leaders to face the challenges of an ever-changing world. The authors tackle the range of issues leaders face offering biblical and practical advice stemming from years of experience. Whether you are an established leader or just beginning, this book will help you to identify what Christian leadership is about. Busy church leaders will find it an excellent resource for developing new members of the team. Emerging leaders will be encouraged by the honest and relevant approach.

> *"Good and godly leadership is the critical need for the church of Jesus Christ in every continent. Some leaders may have special natural abilities but all who engage in leadership of any sort can learn to be better and more effective leaders. This book makes a valuable contribution to leadership training, building on a firm biblical foundation and containing wise advice and practical guidelines for any who take this role in the local church and also in any form of Christian ministry. It is highly recommended."* — Ian Burness, former General Director, Echoes International mission agency

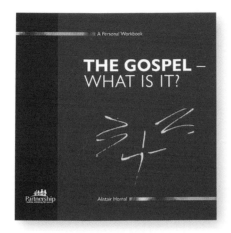

THE GOSPEL: WHAT IS IT?
Personal workbook

By Alistair Hornal
Paperback with page-marker flaps
72 pages RRP £4.99

ISBN 9781916013056

There is nothing more important for Christians to believe. Nothing is more essential for the world to hear. Yet – amazingly – even Bible-loving Christians don't always agree on what the gospel is. Some even seem to drive a wedge between the gospel Jesus preached and the gospel found in the rest of the New Testament.

This workbook explores a range of biblical teaching on the gospel, from Jesus in the Gospels, Paul's letters, early Christian preaching as well as the Old Testament. It offers a united understanding of the gospel – centred on Jesus. It enables you to come to your own conclusions, setting a course for a lifetime of discovery of the riches of the Good News of God.